William Gumede

RESTLESS NATION

Making Sense of Troubled Times

Tafelberg

Tafelberg
An imprint of NB Publishers,
40 Heerengracht, Cape Town
www.tafelberg.com
© William Gumede (2012)

Cover design: John McCann
Book design: Nazli Jacobs
Editing: James Woodhouse and Linde Dietrich
Proofreading: Glynne Newlands

Printed and bound by Interpak Books, Pietermaritzburg
Product group from well-managed forests and other controlled sources.
First edition, first impression 2012
Second impression 2012

ISBN: 978-0-624-05592-1

Epub: 978-0-624-05593-8

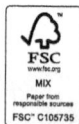

FSC
www.fsc.org
MIX
Paper from
responsible sources
FSC® C105735

To the memory of Patrick van Sleight (1971-2008). *Hamba kahle.* And to the unsung heroes of the 1985 youth generation: building the inclusive, democratic and caring South African society we dreamed of then, is so much more exasperating, painful and complex than we could have ever imagined. Yet, we cannot give up on that dream.

About the author

WILLIAM GUMEDE is an honorary associate professor at the Graduate School of Public and Development Management at the University of the Witwatersrand, a contributing comment writer for *The Guardian*; and a former deputy editor of the *Sowetan*.

Other books by the author

Thabo Mbeki and the Battle for the Soul of the ANC (2005)

The Poverty of Ideas: South African Democracy and the Retreat of the Intellectuals (co-editor with Leslie Dikeni, 2009)

A Kite's Flight (children's book, 2010)

Forthcoming

The Democracy Gap: Africa's Wasted Years

That's better! (children's book, 2012)

Contents

Author's note

These are selected columns, blogs and written and radio opinion pieces. They appeared or were aired after 2005. A full collection, including my substantial work before that, would span many books. The commentary included in this collection tries to make sense of these increasingly uncertain, complex and dangerous times, and the astonishingly self-interested and empty leadership at the head of our society. Our leadership seems bereft of any fresh ideas, or, if not that, are either appallingly complacent or simply lacking the will to steer SA Inc to surer ground.

Sadly, in the rest of Africa and worldwide, for that matter, there appears to be the same leadership vacuum. Some of these pieces were edited and shortened for length. In some cases, the original version of the commentary was used when it was substantially reduced in the published version. These commentaries have all appeared in media with very specific audiences – and sometimes quite specialist – and have not always been generally available, at home or abroad. The intention of this publication is to bring this commentary to a much wider audience.

William Gumede
Johannesburg

The leadership paralysis in the ANC

The limits of a liberation legacy

The inability to transform from resistance movements into effective governing parties lies at the heart of the governmental failures of many African independence and liberation movements. Such movements, of which the African National Congress (ANC) is a case in point, come to power with an extraordinary amount of legitimacy, given their history of opposing colonial governments or white minority regimes.

This 'struggle legitimacy' gives them a much stronger political, economic and moral mandate than that of governments in most other developing countries (except some in East Asia that have also emerged from colonial domination). Their social capital gives them the ability to mobilise societies behind their programmes for long periods, without serious challenges to their legitimacy. But, if such power goes unchecked, it also means that they can get away with service delivery failure, autocratic behaviour and wrongdoing in the name of advancing the liberation or independence project.

Members, supporters and voters are extraordinarily lenient to these movements and they, in turn, have extraordinary power to bestow legitimacy on individuals, institutions and behaviour. Conversely, their struggle credentials also allow them to delegitimise individuals, institutions or behaviour, of which they disapprove. In power, they have an additional legitimising tool: the new state and its apparatus. Combined, if used for the widest possible national, public good and democratic interest, this legitimacy should arguably be a powerful tool for African independence and liberation movements turned government to transform their societies for the better. Yet, most such movements have, once in power, squandered this opportunity.

Because they have such hegemony, the political culture that is manifested within these movements is also replicated within the new state. In their attempts to transform their societies, leaders of these movements fuse their parties with the new state to form a kind of 'party state', with the movement and the party becoming almost indistinguishable. There is no firewall between the party itself and the executive, legislatures and public institutions. In fact, independent democratic institutions are seen as an extension of the party, and not only are the heads of such institutions 'deployed' by the party leadership, they are also expected to defer to it.

The difficulty for many African countries is how to reverse the negative impact on the state if the political culture of the dominant movement turns undemocratic, autocratic or authoritarian. Given the nature of the independence and liberation struggles, these movements are organised in a top-down, secretive and military-like fashion, with power in the hands of a small leadership group. When the leadership decides, the members are expected to obey according to the principle of democratic centralism.

Most independence and liberation movements which are still in power see their movements as the embodiment of the 'people' and therefore see themselves as able to speak for the whole nation, with the leader as the tribune of the 'people'. Typically, during their liberation struggles, nations were divided between those on the side of the liberation movement and those that were aligned with the colonial or minority government or their allies. In power, many independence and liberation movements still divide the world between those on their side and those belonging to the old order. Opposition or criticism, whether from within or from outside the movement, is therefore often wrongly construed as 'opposition' to the demands of the 'people'. The result of such reasoning has been that independence and liberation movements rarely feel obliged to own up to their failures or examine themselves.

The ANC seems to have fallen into this trap as well. Former ANC secretary-general, and now deputy president, Kgalema Motlanthe's famous report on the state of the movement's internal organisation and values has spoken volumes about such behaviour. To realign itself with its original mission, the challenge for the ANC would be to face up to Motlanthe's call to transform itself from the inside out. Its members, supporters and activists should play a more active role in keeping the ANC democratic and holding its leadership accountable.

In South Africa, we are fortunate that a range of other progressive groups also have 'struggle' legitimacy. Some of these movements are outside the ANC family: the Pan Africanist Congress (PAC) and the Black Consciousness Movement (BCM). These movements have, of course, now lost most of their struggle legitimacy as leadership squabbles and weak policies, combined with the ANC's dominance, have contributed to their demise, but importantly, ANC allies, such as the South African Communist Party (SACP) and the Congress of South African Trade Unions (COSATU), have struggle legitimacy in their own right, even though they are in alliance with the ANC.

Moreover, progressive civil society organisations, of which many participated or had their genesis in the United Democratic Front (UDF), can also claim legitimacy from the same source. It is their responsibility to stop the ANC from backsliding into undemocratic behaviour by being assertive civic watchdogs. This role should not be seen as inimical to their alliance with the ANC. Pro-democracy activists from the ANC, together with progressive civil society groups, unions and SACP members could, for example, form a pro-democracy lobby within the ANC that could push for the total internal democratisation of the party at all organisational levels.

But society must also be less tolerant of non-delivery, mismanagement and leaders' autocratic behaviour. The current wave of protest against public representatives should be viewed positively, provided that it stays within the restrictions of the law. It is a form of public criticism which helps to hold the ANC leadership accountable when democratic institutions do not. COSATU General Secretary Zwelinzima Vavi summed it up when he said: 'The election of a progressive leadership [does not] mean the end of the struggle and that we must now step back and hand over everything to these progressive, trusted leaders as though they are messiahs and will deliver everything on a silver platter, while we are in our beds sleeping.'

Individual leaders of the ANC deployed by the party leadership to head independent oversight institutions, such as the Chapter 9 institutions, must become more independent, and serve the public interest and not the interests of the ANC leadership, which do not always coincide. In summary, if a critical mass of individuals, institutions and communities with struggle credentials from within the ANC family are assertive in their dissent when the ANC acts against the public interest, the organisation's leadership is likely to become more accountable and responsive to criticism. At the same time, consistent dismissal of such criticism on the grounds that it is counter-revolutionary will become increasingly difficult to sustain.

In Mauritius (one of the two most successful post-independence African societies with Botswana) the independence movement split in half a decade after independence. The split went right through the middle, not only of the party, but also of the trade unions and civil society groups that were aligned to the movement. Both the old and the breakaway movement had 'struggle' credentials, which meant that the electorate could now choose between two 'legitimate' progressive movements. The problem with the Congress of the People (COPE), which broke away from the ANC, is that, although its members have struggle legitimacy, it has been unable to shake off the perception that it represents the rejected leadership elite of the ANC. Now off course, COPE is engulfed in leadership struggles similar to those that caused the PAC and the BCM to implode.

The mistake that the Democratic Alliance (DA) made in the past is that it did not position itself as a liberation movement, albeit a 'liberal' one. Its policy and leadership positioning in the past reinforced the perception among the black majority that it defended the interests of a white minority or the apartheid order. Now in power in the Western Cape, the DA has the opportunity to show that it can be an alternative but relevant party which can not only govern better but also more inclusively. It must be able to show that service delivery to the black communities in the Western Cape will in five years be better at all levels than in provinces run by the ANC.

COPE can build on its struggle legitimacy if it repositions itself as a party for the black poor rather than the middle class, and if it uses the next five years to build a real presence in poor, working-class black communities.

The mandate President Jacob Zuma received is not ironclad: South African society is restless, and the credibility of the ANC may be wearing thin in the face of increasing delivery deficits, dashed expectations and an inability to communicate the reasons behind this state of affairs. These factors, combined with increasing economic hardships relating to the effects of the global financial crisis, could yet threaten the ANC's struggle legitimacy, the main reason for its electoral success.

SA Reconciliation Barometer, Vol. 7, Issue 2, *August 2009*

The ANC has much to be proud of on its birthday, but little to celebrate

As the ANC celebrates its centenary, the party has much to look back on with pride. Compared with other African liberation movements, the ANC had the unique ability to unite diverse groups. The others were formed on the basis of one ethnic or regional group, and could never transcend this; the ANC created a broad alliance that spanned the ideological spectrum, from shopkeepers to communists. It became what was called a 'multi-class' organisation.

Furthermore, the ANC turned the struggle against apartheid into a moral struggle – and a global one. By the 1980s the ANC had formed links with groups ranging from churches and youth groups in the West and developing world, to ruling powers in the Eastern bloc. The ANC also produced pragmatic and visionary leaders with global appeal, such as Nelson Mandela and Albert Luthuli (the first African to receive the Nobel prize for peace).

The ANC's armed struggle did not dominate every aspect of the movement, as it did in Zimbabwe's ZANU-PF or Angola's MPLA. In the ANC there were democratic forces that opposed the domination of a violent guerrilla culture. In the main, the ANC's operation ethos, whether in exile or in prisons such as Robben Island, genuinely attempted to emphasise internal democracy – consultation, inclusiveness, freedom of expression and the right to dissent – even if there were some appalling incidents to the contrary.

But as the ANC reaches its 100th birthday, antidemocratic groups appear to have a stranglehold on the party. Key ANC leaders wrote South Africa's post-apartheid Constitution – which set out a clear democratic, human rights and values framework for a new South Africa. Today, incredibly, some leaders are saying that the Constitution, particularly its freedom of expression provisions, 'undermines' development.

The intelligence and security forces, as well as the police, are routinely used in ANC leadership battles to trip up political rivals. Even corruption appears to be sometimes selectively prosecuted to sideline opponents. The cloak-and-dagger style of operations of the rogue elements of the ANC's military and intelligence wings has now become dominant within the party.

One of the fundamental clauses in the ANC's guiding 'strategy and tactics' document says members 'must be informed by the values of honesty, hard work, humility, service to the people and respect for the laws of the land'. The current reality is embarrassingly opposite. This is illustrated in the contrast between the moral authority of a Mandela, an Oliver Tambo or a Luthuli – all former presidents of the ANC – and the murkiness of a Jacob Zuma, who is seeking re-election as party leader this year.

In his 2007 campaign to become leader, many Zuma supporters were 100% Zulu in their support for the man from KwaZulu-Natal. Out of the window went the inclusive, non-tribal and nonracial ethos of the ANC's long struggle. The ANC Women's League backed Zuma's leadership bid even after he claimed he knew a woman wanted sex with him because she didn't cross her legs.

Increasingly, top leaders in the ANC are chosen by small cliques – selected for how best they can balance factional and patronage interests. ANC leaders talk about efforts to tackle poverty, yet wastage of public resources and conspicuous consumption by elected officials have rocketed. The ANC in government runs the risk of making the same mistake as other failed African liberation movements – enriching the few, mostly those who are politically connected, rather than the poor masses.

Despite all this, the ANC is likely to be in power for some time. Opposition parties at the moment are perceived to be largely irrelevant, too disorganised or too white. There is, of course, the possibility that disillusioned sections of the ANC can break away. However, most supporters will be reluctant to do so given the miserable performance of the most recent splinter group, COPE.

The lack of a credible challenger encourages complacency in the ANC – with leaders perceiving no reason to shape up. However, with the party seemingly assured of victory in elections for the foreseeable future, largely paying lip service to the values that sustained it for a century, South Africa will struggle to reach its full potential – of becoming a global example for genuine democracy, equitable economic development and peaceful racial integration –

unless truly democratic groups quickly take control of the ANC and steer it back to its roots.

The Guardian, 6 January 2012

ANC leadership battles should be open and democratic

Much of the infighting in the ANC, which is paralysing both government and the party, is the result of outdated codes, traditions and rituals governing the elections of leaders of the party, especially the president.

The opacity in internal ANC elections opens the system to manipulation, corruption and the abuse of state institutions such as the intelligence services, the police and the judiciary, and also raises the possibility of selective prosecutions to sideline rivals. Because of this opacity, incumbents and dominant factions can rewrite and manipulate the rules to favour their leadership campaigns and to undermine opponents.

The problem faced by many African liberation movements is that the top leadership is usually selected by very small cliques and presented to branches and national conferences for rubber-stamping. The leadership candidates are usually presented as one slate of candidates (if you vote for one candidate you are forced to vote for all the other candidates on the slate of that specific candidate) with the preferred presidential leader at the head (in some cases a two-slate system was allowed). These practices usually stem from a time

19

when these movements operated as clandestine opposition parties, when such practices were defended as preventing disunity and
fostering cohesion. In many cases, including that of the ANC, such
non-democratic practices continue – even now that these movements are in government. This devalues democracy.

President Jacob Zuma and ANC General Secretary Gwede Mantashe have banned all public talk about the leadership succession
in the party, saying such talk is premature. Yet the reality is that almost every political manoeuvre by the ANC leadership now is aimed
at influencing the direction of the party's leadership election at the
2012 national elective conference in Bloemfontein.

No matter what one's views are of ANC Youth League leader
Julius Malema, it is fair to say that if he still supported a second term
for Zuma it is most unlikely he would have been suspended. Some
kind of face-saving compromise would have been cobbled together.

Zuma says he would 'never defy' a nomination for a second term
as ANC and South African president. Meanwhile, one has to be politically blind not to see he is running a tough and determined
campaign. The other day, Deputy President Kgalema Motlanthe
unexpectedly issued a statement that as a 'loyal and disciplined
member of the ANC' he is 'not involved in any campaigning or lobbying for the presidency of the ANC', but meanwhile others are running spirited campaigns on his behalf.

Worse, since the 2007 Polokwane conference, presidential candidates are mobilised around a slate of candidates to the ANC's
National Executive Committee (NEC). Then, in 2007, the slate was
limited to one for the then president Thabo Mbeki and the other
for Zuma, with one candidate for each position on either the Mbeki
or the Zuma slate. This meant that individuals were not elected
on merit but on the basis of their allegiances. In such a situation,

mediocre candidates are usually elected to key senior positions in the ANC.

It is likely that the ANC's 2012 leadership election will be decided on slates, probably two only: one slate for a second presidential term for Zuma, the other against. But democracy within the ANC and in the country generally would be better served if the ANC democratised the way it elects leaders.

The very obvious problem with the current system of internal elections in the ANC is that elected presidential and other leadership candidates will always have their mandates questioned. Losing groups will always feel afterwards that the winning candidates won unfairly. The winners will continually be challenged by those who lose out, especially in situations such as that now faced by the ANC, where the winning slate monopolises state patronage, positions and business deals, and could even hound those on the losing slate out of the party.

Democratising the ANC's presidential elections would therefore bring better leaders to the fore. There is a higher premium on quality leaders in infant democracies such as South Africa, where democratic institutions, political cultures and nation-building efforts are still nascent, and where undemocratic leaders can damage the system.

Among the worst failings of the system of African liberation movements, whereby leaders are chosen by small cliques, is that the most talented, those with the best ideas, especially young leaders from outside the old patronage networks, are almost never elected to the top leadership. This is because the cliques that supervise elections fear they may shake up existing, lucrative patronage networks. In fact, in most cases the leaders chosen by such small cliques in these liberation movements are not selected for their

21

holistic leadership qualities, such as the ability to bring new ideas to the party and the country, but for how best they can balance factional interests.

Thus, African liberation movements may have quality leaders but they almost never rise to the presidency. The criteria for leadership nomination are narrowly delineated and produce leaders who may have struggle credentials but little skill in leading complex and changing societies. In the environment of increasing global uncertainty, and in a world driven by fast-changing technology, the certainties of the past cannot offer a reliable guide to the future. The existing system favours patriarchy and older leaders, or it favours younger leaders who mimic the old in their thinking and behaviour. Partly as a result of this phenomenon, very few African countries since independence have been able to elect more dynamic new leaders.

South Africa's democracy would be much enhanced if the ANC were to introduce the idea of American-style party primaries into its presidential election campaign, with presidential hopefuls going directly to both the ANC membership and their own supporters, making a case for why they should be elected as president.

Groups within the tripartite alliance – trade unions, civic groups, communists – could nominate candidates. A period could then be set for campaigning and defending manifestos. All party members could then vote. All parties receiving public money should be required to prove that their internal elections are conducted in ways that are in keeping with the democratic norms of South Africa's Constitution.

More broadly, and moving beyond the internal elections of parties such as the ANC, South Africa's current electoral system of proportional representation should be changed to a constituency-based system. This would make members of parliament, legislatures and local government directly accountable to those in their constituencies who elected them, not to party leaders, as is now the case.

COSATU, in a prescient argument in a 2006 discussion paper, said that the current system 'undermines independent thought', because individual careers depend on endorsement by the party leadership and by the ANC deployment committee. The document argued that unless the system changes, 'the movement towards sycophancy is inevitable'. Proportional representation reinforces the party's power to make or break the careers of independent-minded leaders, even if they are competent. It makes it possible to protect leaders who are incompetent but who are perceived to be loyal to the party leader.

Both the Mbeki and Zuma presidencies have ignored the very useful proposals made by a government task team appointed in 2002 to investigate the most suitable electoral system for South Africa. The team, led by the late Frederik van Zyl Slabbert, proposed that three quarters of the current 400 MPs be elected on the basis of a constituency system. Such a system would increase accountability in our electoral system, allowing communities to elect their representatives directly and to recall them if they are felt to be failing that community.

This far into South Africa's post-1994 democracy, voters, especially ANC members and supporters, have simply stayed away from the polls if they are unhappy with the party. Many ANC members and supporters view other parties as inadequate. A vote means little if opposition parties are weak – the norm in many poorly governed African and developing countries.

Perhaps we could add to every South African ballot paper a box

23

that gives voters the opportunity to vote for none of the parties on the ballot paper. In this way, they can still exercise their vote while expressing their disapproval of the quality of all the political parties and leaders up for election.

Mail & Guardian, 15 December 2011

The sources of Malema's power

Why is it that President Jacob Zuma and most of the ANC leadership appear to be currently held prisoner by ANC Youth League President Julius Malema? The source of Malema's power is that he played a leading role in helping to oust President Thabo Mbeki from the leadership of the ANC and the country. Malema helped rally significant sections of the ANC behind Zuma in his successful battle with Mbeki for control of the ANC. This means that Zuma owes Malema a gigantic political favour.

In addition to this, the Youth League, with its thousands of members, many of whom are idle, are a useful press gang to be mobilised for campaigns, protests and rallies. Throughout Zuma's rape trial, corruption hearings and fights with Mbeki, they almost daily embarked on mass protests, helping to convey the impression that support for Zuma was an unstoppable 'tsunami'.

Furthermore, in the run-up to the battle of Polokwane, Youth Leaguers, during branch polls, flooded ANC meetings, increasing voting numbers and influencing results. At ANC branch level, voting mostly operates with a show of hands in public and a faction that floods a meeting with a block of voters can easily swing the outcome.

New terms of political engagement emerged in the battle for control of the ANC between Zuma and Mbeki. Both groups on occasion used underhand means, whether selectively leaking confidential information, or using state institutions, such as the intelligence agencies, to trip up adversaries. Vote buying became a norm – money has now become so important in ANC political contests that a presidential candidate without a massive war chest, whether drawn from state coffers or private donors, has a very slim chance of success.

This kind of undemocratic political culture is now entrenched within the ANC family and the Youth League is a formidable force in the context of this new political environment. For Zuma and the current ANC leadership, who came to power with the help of the Youth League, it now becomes difficult to ask the proponents of these tactics to desist.

Given Malema and the ANC Youth League's success in ousting Mbeki, many senior ANC figures with presidential ambitions now see the Youth League as important foot soldiers in their proxy presidential battles and generously fund its leaders in order to woo them. Malema himself, a wily operator, appears to play candidates off according to who can offer the most generous financial terms or can best advance his political career. He clearly sees himself as a contender for the ANC presidency in the future and this fact now influences all his decisions. And in the eyes of many ANC members, Zuma crowned him as a future president of the ANC when he announced last year that Malema was 'presidential' material. This undoubtedly raised Malema's stock in the ANC.

But Malema's power also lies elsewhere. Traditionally, the ANC Youth League has always been given the latitude to be contrary and Malema's power lies in the fact that the controversial views he expresses are at least partially resonant with significant numbers of black South Africans. If he calls for nationalisation, the truth is that there is widespread anger that redistribution to the poor has not worked. Of course, the answer is not traditional nationalisation, but finding ways to make existing government departments and state-owned enterprises work more efficiently – by reducing cronyism, doing away with jobs for pals and encouraging business to be more proactive in terms of job creation and skills transfer. However, this does not mean that Malema's views do not resonate with many people.

The youth of South Africa are significant in electoral terms. Statistics tell us that they are likely to be unemployed; poor and without hope; resentful of both the white establishment and the new black elite. The ANC leadership has problems reaching out to them, but Malema has managed to become their spokesperson – they can identify with him because he is like them (he is the embodiment of black marginalised youth: poor education, no job except for working for the ANC). But more than this, he is an inspiration – he has moved from rural poverty to a life of fine clothes, fast cars and expensive whiskies.

Beeld, 28 June 2010

Putting the people's needs over the leaders' wants

Given the extreme poverty of the majority of ordinary South Africans, it is an affront that political leaders elected after promising to change the lives of the poor live in extraordinary opulence on public money.

The majority of South Africans are living without jobs, houses and food. They have given the ANC a mandate to lift them out of this grinding poverty as quickly as possible. Given this situation, our leaders must start to live modestly. Some political activists, during the past election, were driving Hummers while campaigning in squatter camps, urging poverty-stricken people who do not know where their next meal will come from to vote for them. This really is an insult to the majority of South Africans who struggle to make ends meet in these tough economic times.

Elected leaders are living the high life on taxpayers' money, and in their bubble of luxury they are forgetting about the poor. Jacob Zuma must change the culture of opulence so pervasive in government. For starters, Zuma must ban extravagant 'blue-light' convoys, where one minister is transported in a large convoy of cars driving at breakneck speed, pushing other ordinary motorists and pedestrians off the road.

The crowd of security guards that surround ministers must be cut down to one per minister. It is a disgrace that they are surrounded by so many bodyguards, while an ordinary citizen in Soweto must face the brunt of daily crime, without bodyguards or responsive police, without the money to buy expensive private security.

Better still, leaders must start to use public transport. Ken Livingstone, the former mayor of London in the United Kingdom, took the bus and the train to work and meetings every day. This also made him more accessible to ordinary citizens who could vent their anger at lack of delivery at him in person.

If local politicians take minibus taxis, trains and buses every day, they will experience first-hand the daily dance of death that ordinary citizens experience using public transport.

Leaders must also drive more humble cars. Imagine President Zuma decreeing that all ANC-elected public officials should drive less expensive official cars, say cars costing under R200 000. Leaders must also live modestly.

Elected leaders must live in the constituency areas which they represent. This means that if they represent Soweto, they must live there. This will also ensure that they are reminded daily of the hardships and poverty of ordinary South Africans. This will also make them immediately accessible to the ordinary citizens they claim to represent.

Elected public officials must behave with more humility. President Zuma must issue an instruction that ministers should no longer be addressed as 'Your Excellency' or 'The Honourable'; instead the president should instruct all his ministers to address ordinary citizens in this way. This should help install a culture of elected officials who are there to serve citizens. Ministers must stand in queues in shops like ordinary citizens – there should be no jumping of queues because the person is a minister or a 'VIP'.

Secondly, all VIP areas at public events that are funded by taxpayers must be banned. Leaders must mingle with ordinary people. Furthermore, extravagant parties for publicly elected officials that are funded by taxpayers should be banned. So too must the huge banquets available at meetings of government officials. This will save taxpayers huge amounts of money which can then be redirected to poverty-alleviation projects.

Excessive bonuses in the public sector should be curtailed. In many state-owned companies executives give themselves performance bonuses when they have managed failing and loss-making institutions. This must stop.

President Zuma has a golden opportunity to bring accountability to South Africa's political system. Elected leaders who do not deliver must be fired, especially if they are close allies and friends of the president. Under Mbeki, the most incompetent deployees were never fired if they were slavishly loyal to the president. Zuma's proposal to open a direct line to him, where ordinary citizens can complain about poor service delivery, corruption and indifference, is a good idea, but what matters is whether action will be taken against callous government officials following complaints by ordinary citizens.

Sowetan, 16 July 2009

Has the ANC become a tenderpreneur?

What is happening to South Africa's ANC and its leadership? There can be no doubt that if the ruling party is a shareholder in a private company that tenders for state contracts this represents a clear conflict of interest.

The ANC has a financial arm, Chancellor House, which owns a 25% stake in Hitachi Power Africa. Hitachi has been awarded a contract by Eskom, the electricity utility, to supply and install boilers for power stations. The ANC's stake in the deal through Chancellor

House was estimated in 2008 to be R5,8 billion. For the sake of transparency, accountability and clean governance there has to be a firewall between the ruling political party and its leaders, on the one hand, and state and private companies, on the other. It is hardly unlikely that when a company that is partially owned by the ANC is bidding for a government or parastatal tender, such a company will not be awarded the contract.

Soon after the ANC's national conference in December 2007, the then newly minted party treasurer Mathews Phosa promised, as part of a post-Polokwane spring-cleaning, to disinvest the party's shares in Hitachi. This has not happened. The ANC must do so, and it must close down Chancellor House.

Good ruling parties govern in the broadest public interest. Private companies have a narrow motive – that of expressly securing a profit for their shareholders. They rarely work for the benefit of the public interest. It would be a shame if the ANC leadership governs in a way that maximises its profits in its investments, rather than maximising the prosperity of the whole of SA Inc.

If the party is a major shareholder in Hitachi, how can one be certain that the ANC leadership applied their minds objectively in the proposed 35% tariff hike proposed by Eskom? The tariff increase is likely to hit the struggling economy, families and businesses at the worst possible moment. Ultimately, ordinary black South Africans – the ANC's bedrock constituency – are going to suffer the most.

To get our economy back on an even keel demands tough choices, difficult trade-offs and decisions. Some of these will no doubt be very painful. Knowing such decisions are taken with the best long-term interests of the country at heart, rather than for the profit of a few individuals, makes such choices more palatable.

Similarly, to award state contracts for critical services to black economic empowerment (BEE) companies on the basis of their owners' political connections or liberal donations to the ANC, while knowing that they do not have the capacity to deliver, and so again robbing the poor of 'a better life', is equally wrong. It is unacceptable that state-owned companies disburse finance or tenders to businesses linked to their own board of directors. It is just silly for someone to say, 'I recused myself from the meeting where the decision was made.' Neither is it enough for state-owned companies to say they have disclosed such transactions in annual reports. The point is: If your friends and comrades are on the board that will make the decision to award a tender to your company, you do not need to be physically there.

Ultimately, we also need to bring greater transparency to the funding of political parties. Knowing which companies or individuals have donated to the ANC, DA or COPE is almost the only way to know whether they have secured their tenders solely on the basis of this, rather than merit. Almost every African liberation and independence movement lost the plot when they, or individual leaders, started to dabble in business, securing state tenders and contracts, trying to make profit, for themselves or the party leadership, rather than at all times governing in the broadest public interest.

Sowetan, 28 January 2010

Doublespeak paralyses society and the economy

If one listens to public statements from many senior ANC-COSATU-SACP tripartite alliance leaders, one cannot help but notice that doublespeak has now – sadly – become the dominant culture. Leaders say one thing, but do the opposite. Some leaders say they are pro-poor, but they drive R1,2-million cars paid for with public money. Others call for strong measures against corruption, but behave in dodgy ways themselves. And yet others defend gender equality while in the same breath making outrageously sexist statements.

Some argue for nationalisation of the mines, saying that this will redistribute resources to the poor. If only this was genuine. In reality, they want to bail out struggling BEE tycoons or put their friends in charge of the proposed nationalised companies – and so extend their web of patronage. Others defend our democratic institutions, but in their actions undermine them. They defend the rule of law and call for those who transgress it to be harshly punished. Yet, they themselves – as senior politicians – appear to be untouchable. When they do wrong, they can manipulate things in such a way that they will go scot-free.

Leaders 'talk left, but act right'. Some say they are communists, but their real actions indicate they are not. In public ANC leaders say everything is hunky-dory, that they are 'united', but in private they fight viciously among themselves. Nobody knows any more what the genuine policies of leaders and organisations within the ANC family are.

It is now difficult to distinguish between fact and fantasy. It is a circus. If the consequences were not so tragic, one could joke about it. Firstly, the policy confusion that the double talk is causing means that those who devise and implement policies either do not have adequate information, or have the wrong information, to do so effectively. The same goes for those who want to make new investments. They cannot do so, because they do not know the real policy position of government.

Mixed messages from politicians make it very difficult for government planners to allocate resources efficiently. They also cause implementation paralysis. Senior civil servants are reluctant to implement policies they are not sure are backed by the influential politicians in the ANC. It could be career-ending.

The double talk also opens the door for corruption. Since there is no certainty about policies, those with enough money can pay to have policies that favour their interests implemented.

Ordinary people are totally confused. Government leaders make outrageous promises, even if they know the resources are not available (not to mention the capacity). They talk up the expectations of ordinary citizens. Not surprisingly, promises made this way are hardly ever met fully. No wonder that many deflated communities then vent their frustration in angry outbursts by burning down municipal buildings, trains and the homes of local elected representatives.

It is better if there is total honesty about policies. It is also better to state the real motivation for particular decisions and approaches. Then society can debate the various proposals on their merits and honestly decide our core priorities – which we cannot do effectively now, in a culture where doublespeak is the norm.

If only for selfish reasons, the ANC, COSATU and the SACP must stop the doublespeak. It erodes the trust their members and supporters have in them, and without that trust their membership will leave them sooner rather than later. Importantly, ordinary citizens will become more cynical and withdraw from politics altogether, or start to express their preferences increasingly violently.

Sowetan, 21 January 2010

Riding out the storm of political uncertainty

Developing countries that have prospered since the Second World War have generally had focused political leadership at the helm. After the ANC's National General Council (NGC) in Durban recently it must now be clear that the people leading South Africa don't necessarily possess this quality. In fact, it is obvious that the ANC's leadership has lost direction.

The ANC's NGC deferred all critical policy decisions until the national conference in 2012, which means South Africa will have more of the same until then – loud bickering between the ANC's different factions over policy – which will continue to paralyse government. And if Jacob Zuma succeeds in his bid for another five-year term, this cycle of paralysis will likely be repeated.

For the past two years it appears that whatever positive developments, whether new investment or outbursts of national unity during the Soccer World Cup, happened not because of the quality of our political leadership, but rather, in spite of its paucity. Can South Africa prosper when its leadership is weak, disorganised and inept? And can those outside politics make any difference?

Firstly, it is very rare for a developing country to advance economically unless the political leadership in charge is focused. Over the last 50 years we have seen many developing countries – in Latin America, Africa, the Middle East and Southeast Asia – with high economic growth rates where the benefits of this growth have not been reinvested productively, because the political leadership only looked after themselves or simply lacked the depth to give direction.

In most advanced democracies the democratic institutions are strong and generally independent. Furthermore, politics at municipal level is quite often independent from national politics and municipal leaders are in power because they deliver on local issues, rather than because they hold allegiance to the governing party. In many cases local governments can raise taxes, and are mandated to deliver public services such as education, health, water and energy at a local level.

Italy is an example of a country which has a legacy of poor political leadership. Yet the country's public service is relatively independent from the ruling political party and is meritocratic. Italy's public service. Italy's public service is also ring-fenced – public servants remain in their jobs no matter which party is in power – and this means that high-quality public services can still be delivered even if those leading the country are inept and corrupt or, as is often the case in Italy, there are rapid changes in government.

Furthermore, nongovernmental sectors in Italy – business, civil society, the press and academia – are generally aggressively independent, and continue to function no matter which party is in power. And although the judiciary and the police have been criticised regularly in recent years, there are huge pockets of excellence that, ultimately, compensate for the corrupt elements, and make the overall system function.

How does contemporary South Africa compare? Within the ANC there are obvious differences over policy and the resultant administrative paralysis will continue until the party has its national conference in December 2012. The irony, of course, is that the ANC is a single entity but operates as if it were different parties with different policies. South Africa has poor-quality political leadership and most of the public service and state-owned company sectors are inefficient because they have more often than not become places of patronage for the elite of the ruling party. And because critical appointments are mostly dependent on the ruling party, and sometimes even the faction in control, a change at the top also means a turnover of management. Consequently, the public service in South Africa does not offer a buffer for misguided decisions from inept political leaders. On top of this, every changeover appears to bring in new policies. The implementation of policy is therefore constantly interrupted and in such a context it becomes near impossible to plan for the long term, which is crucial to ensure prosperity.

In South Africa's case, pockets of excellence in the public service and state-owned companies operate side by side with less effective structures. Such pockets include the Treasury, the Reserve Bank, the Revenue Service, the Industrial Development Corporation (IDC) and the Development Bank of Southern Africa (DBSA). Some public service departments and state-owned companies may not be centres of excellence, but they function reasonably well – Eskom and Transnet, for instance. There are also centres of excellence among some of South Africa's regulatory bodies, such as the Office of the Auditor-General. Others, such as the Commission for Gender Equality and the Independent Communications Authority of SA (ICASA), are appallingly ineffective.

What counts in South Africa's favour is that it has many pockets of excellence outside the governmental sphere – which is not the case in many developing countries. Even if the public sector is erratic, the private sector equivalents – providing health care and education, for example – can compete with the best in the world. Furthermore, South Africa has private sector companies, nongovernmental organisations and civil groups that are highly effective – the latter ranging from organisations like the Institute for Democracy in Africa (IDASA) to the Treatment Action Campaign (TAC).

One way for South Africa to ride out the current storm of political uncertainty, at least in the short term, is for the pockets of excellence in the public and private sectors to step into the breach. In the absence of coherent political leadership the centres of excellence in the public and private sectors, as well as in civil society, will have to provide leadership. For example, in May 2010 South Africa's two largest business organisations, Business Leadership South Africa and Business Unity South Africa, pledged to come up with self-generated initiatives to help government increase electricity capacity. Or Business Leadership South Africa's initiative to triple the size of South Africa's economy within a generation. Or their initiative to get CEOs to commit to skills development and more responsible corporate behaviour.

Companies, of course, have to focus on maximising returns for shareholders. However, in our context companies must also be better corporate citizens. Rather than pursuing narrow black economic empowerment, to enrich a few black individuals in the right faction, adopt 100 of the poorest black schools – the benefits will be so much greater.

The investment arms of COSATU-affiliated trade unions have billions in their kitties. This money can, for example, be used to make more ethical and productive investments, rather than funding

37

narrow BEE enterprises. Other COSATU affiliates must follow the Southern African Clothing and Textile Workers' Union (SACTWU) and the National Union of Mineworkers (NUM) in organising winter schools and bursaries for the children of their members and skills training for workers who have been retrenched.

But what can individuals do?

Efforts such as the launch of the Council for the Advancement of the South African Constitution (CASAC) by prominent South Africans are crucial to defending our democratic rights. Furthermore, it is crucial that individuals and nongovernmental organisations continue to express their outrage at the proposed media tribunal, which would allow the state to regulate the media, and the information bill, which would in practice hinder public awareness of official corruption and wrongdoing.

The instinctive reaction of many who care about their country is to turn inwards at a time such as this. However, what South Africa needs right now is for individuals to become more involved in their communities, whether it is sitting on school boards, attending the meetings of local municipalities (and challenging the councillors there) or supporting community organisations and charities. Ideally, we want government to actually do its job, but this kind of public mobilisation can fill the gap when government fails.

Furthermore, individuals who are members and supporters of political parties must hold their leaders to account. ANC members should do more to make their party more responsible; members of opposition parties must do more to make them more relevant.

Lastly, in the absence of responsible political leadership, corporate, civil and church leaders must fill the vacuum.

Beeld, 1 October 2010

ANC must spring-clean, nothing less

These are unsettling times. Among both black and white South Africans there is a paralysing feeling of anxiety, drift and imminent collapse. This in itself damages the economy because many, especially in the public sector, feel that their hard work will be cancelled out by those greedily eating away scarce public resources. There is a choking sense that the current generation in government may not have the ideas or political will to lead us out of this malaise.

Many supporters of the ANC also wonder whether we will be struck by that curse of African liberation movements – the failure to improve the lot of the widest number of people and to create a better and caring society. This is a cataclysmic shift in the political climate. Are there any solutions?

There are new task teams, calls for more debate on morality, new laws . . . But with no urgent amendment of the electoral law to allow citizens to elect their representatives directly, rather than for party leaders to choose them, these will be band-aid measures. This crisis has deep institutional, moral and leadership dimensions, and only a spring-clean of leadership, ideas and institutions will lift the gloom.

In most democratic societies the obvious way out of such stagnation is an electoral solution. This is not realistic in our case. The opposition parties are too limited and the ANC is too dominant.

The alternative is for the ANC itself to spring-clean. This will mean making itself more democratic, transparent and responsive. It will demand political courage, will and resolve from the ANC's leadership, and a change of culture – as any ANC leader who championed a shake-up of the party in the current climate would be likely to have their career killed off.

The ANC desperately needs a better calibre of leadership at all levels. Amilcar Cabral, one of the great thinkers of African liberation ideology, said the success of liberation movements that become governments depends on the personal moral behaviour, decency and honesty of their leaders and members. Cabral argued that these qualities were more important when they were in government than an adherence to ideology and a mechanical dedication to the rules and policies of the party.

Inside the ANC, prospective leaders must be elected on a truly competitive basis. The ANC leadership must open all internal party elections. Candidates must apply openly for all vacancies, as one applies for a job in the private sector. Interviewing panels must be independent, staffed by neutral veterans, or even independent outsiders with status. Candidates must be judged on the basis of merit, moral character and commitment to public service. This will help to bring fresh blood into the party.

The policy of African leadership must be done away with, because it is being manipulated. If Trevor Manuel, for example, is the best candidate for the ANC presidency, he must be elected as the ANC president. In the public sector, appointments to senior government positions, state-owned enterprises and commissions must be opened up beyond the ANC membership pool, across colour and political affiliations.

Importantly, the system of merit must be applied across the party and the public service. The lack of such a system has not only made these areas less appealing to the talented, it has also allowed the mediocre, by bootlicking the local party strongman, to flourish. It has also meant that independent-mindedness, which is needed to hold elected officials accountable, has been discouraged, because advancement is based on sucking up to authority.

The ANC leadership must rid itself of the most corrupt senior party leaders first. Ministers and public servants who are under-performing, even if they are powerful in the party, must also be sacked.

The reality is that behavioural change among citizens is only going to be fostered if ANC party leaders are seen to follow the rules applicable to everyone else. Flagrant disregard of the new democratic laws by post-apartheid leaders will only encourage the apartheid-era culture of evading the law to persist. There should not be two sets of laws: one for the party aristocracy and another for ordinary citizens. A lifestyle audit of all party leaders and public servants is absolutely crucial – it will also boost public confidence.

Drop black economic empowerment as a policy and give companies BEE points for how much they invest in job creation, black education and housing; and for uplifting the physical and social infrastructure of townships and rural areas, and supporting the five million entrepreneurs in the informal sector.

Honesty must also be restored to the centre of public debate. In a crisis, it is better for any government to stick with core policies, provided these are genuinely in the interest of the whole country, and then resolutely implement them. Doublespeak to try to please everyone will just compound the uncertainty, drift and paralysis.

Only substantial reform at the centre – in party, government and individual behaviour – will inject fresh public confidence and unlock the paralysis. If the ANC leadership continue with 'business as usual' in the face of our current crisis, it will hit the electoral fortunes of the party. If public service delivery remains sluggish, and leaders keep on looting, more and more ANC members and supporters will desert the party.

Doing nothing will continue a negative cycle of waning public trust in the government, which can only lead to more violent community rebellions and more self-enrichment at the top as those in power loot as much and as quickly as possible before the resources dry up. Inevitably, those in the private sector with the talent and money will then either cut their losses in South Africa and run, or eschew public commitment to look after themselves and their families.

Mail & Guardian, 23 March 2010

Where will the ANC be in another 100 years?

More than 100 000 people celebrated the ANC's centenary by attending three days of festivities in Mangaung township, Bloemfontein – the birthplace of South Africa's ruling party. The nature of the celebration mirrored the state of the ANC today. Leaders dressed in the latest fashions were served expensive food and drink in air-conditioned VIP tents while ordinary members sat in the scorching sun with their free bottled water.

President Zuma lit a centenary flame, which is now touring South Africa as a symbol of the fight against apartheid. The South African Post Office released a commemorative stamp to celebrate Africa's oldest liberation movement. But, sadly, the ANC is in danger of having only past glories to celebrate. It seems as if the ANC leadership of today and their values are at odds with the party's rich heritage. The challenges of being in government are threatening to overwhelm them, just as they did other African liberation movements.

A leitmotif that runs through the history of the ANC has been its ability to revitalise itself in times of decline by taking in new progressive groups. This was either done by democrats from within or by the ANC incorporating other democratic movements and in the process transforming itself. In many ways these waves of renewal over the past 100 years showcase the different eras which the ANC has gone through.

The first, the foundation era, started when the ANC was formed in 1912 by a group of black leaders (mostly chiefs, professionals and businessmen) to fight for black rights and freedoms in the new Union of South Africa. In the Anglo-Boer War of 1899-1902 (also called the South African War) the two Boer republics were defeated by the British. In 1910 they were brought together with the two colonial provinces to form the Union of South Africa, but blacks were denied political rights in the new dispensation.

By the time the Union of South Africa came into being, the British had also broken the power of the last of the African kingdoms, and in 1906 suppressed the last organised African rebellion in Zululand – the Bambatha rebellion. On 8 January 1912 the South African Native National Congress was formed at the Wesleyan Church in Waaihoek, Bloemfontein. In 1923 it changed its name to the African National Congress.

The founding leaders of the ANC were lawyers such as Pixley ka Isaka Seme, Richard Msimang and Alfred Mangena, journalists such as Sol Plaatje and religious leaders like the Reverend John Dube. This group of leaders called not only for the emancipation of black South Africans, but also, in the words of Seme, for 'the regeneration of Africa' as a whole.

43

A second era came when the ANC turned to socialism in the 1920s, under the leadership of Josiah Tshangana Gumede and Eddie Khaile, its general secretary. They were the first African members of the SACP leadership and were influenced by the radical revolutions in Europe.

A third era spans the 1930s, when the ANC leadership, again under the presidency of Seme, focused on economic self-realisation and starting societies and businesses for blacks. Thereafter came an era during which the ANC was radicalised by members of the ANC Youth League – the generation of Nelson Mandela, Oliver Tambo and Walter Sisulu. In their 1949 programme of action document they forced the lacklustre ANC leadership of the time to adopt the strategy of mass action. During this era the Freedom Charter was adopted and mass protests, like the Women's March and the mass burning of pass documents, took place.

The late 1960s and early 1970s belonged to the generation of Steve Biko, the leader of the Black Consciousness (BC) movement, which had its roots in the black student movement. Biko argued that blacks had to shake off their inferiority complexes, ingrained by centuries of white oppression, if they were to achieve national liberation. He also called for democratic practices to be at the centre of the anti-apartheid struggle.

The 16 June 1976 Soweto uprising by high school pupils, led by the likes of Tsietsi Mashinini, brought a new radicalism to the ANC. They protested against the introduction of Afrikaans as the compulsory medium of instruction in black schools and were recruited en masse into the ANC, providing the organisation with a new street-smart generation.

Then came the 1980s, which brought two parallel waves within the ANC. First, the idea of the 'intifada' was brought to the organisation by a new generation who were prepared to sacrifice their lives for liberation. They used the slogan 'victory or death'. At the same time there were 'adult' movements like the United Democratic Front (UDF) – an internal umbrella group of civil groups – nongovernmental organisations (NGOs) and black professional associations, the revitalised trade union movement and white issue-based groups that were opposed to apartheid.

Throughout South Africa's history, colonial and apartheid governments ruled blacks through divide-and-conquer tactics in an attempt to make effective black opposition against oppression impossible. Mac Maharaj, transport minister in the cabinet of former president Nelson Mandela, said the ANC's key success was its ability to unify black people against these divisionary tactics. The ANC, through its fierce resistance, gave many blacks a sense of self-worth and a cause. It offered a positive alternative.

The ANC's success as a liberation movement was due to its visionary leadership, its mission to be inclusive of all races, ethnicities and classes, and the fact that it practised inclusive democracy.

In the main, the ANC's internal operation ethos, whether among cadres in exile or political prisoners on Robben Island, was one of consultation, inclusiveness, freedom of expression and the right to dissent. This is not to say that there were not incidences of autocracy or the torture of independently minded members, especially in the exiled armed wing and intelligence structures, or that there were not Stalinist elements, eager to crush dissent, but these were mostly held in check by more democratically minded members.

One of the ANC's biggest successes as a liberation movement was to turn the struggle against apartheid into a moral battle which was fought on a global scale. This strategy was one of the reasons Western churches strongly backed the ANC from the 1980s onwards, generously providing funding and lobbying their governments and congregations to put pressure on the apartheid government.

The ANC produced visionary leaders such as Nelson Mandela, Albert Luthuli and Desmond Tutu. These leaders had moral authority – and by their individual ethical and moral conduct also reinforced the moral dimensions of the struggle. The influence of the church on the ANC during the struggle is often overlooked. In fact, many of the ANC's leaders were deeply influenced by Christianity. They put morality and ethics at the heart of their leadership.

Although started mainly by Africans, the ANC transformed into an organisation which embraced South Africa's diverse communities, including whites. The ANC was also allied to various social, civic, student, traditional and professional organisations. These organisations all influenced the ANC and this helped the movement to avoid becoming ideologically rigid or too narrow in its policy outlook. It was forced to come to terms with diversity, something which time and again helped to revitalise the ANC by providing it with a regular stream of new ideas, leaders and funding.

Historically, the ANC has also been able to successfully incorporate virtually all civil movements and grass-roots activism in South Africa into the party, frequently taking over some of the ideas and campaigns of these organisations and even of its rivals, such as the now almost defunct Pan Africanist Congress (PAC). This has helped the ANC to put itself at the centre of the official history of the South African liberation struggle.

For instance, ANC leaders actively sought to recruit Steve Biko and after his death they lured most of the brightest young talent from the BC movement to the organisation. This generation of black activists and intellectuals, with fresh ideas on genuine participatory democracy, helped the ANC to reach out to a younger, more radical black generation, who at that stage might have perceived the 'old' ANC as irrelevant.

In the 1980s, the organisation brought the new generation of democratic trade unions that had regrouped under the umbrella of COSATU into the ANC fold. It did the same with the 1980s 'civics' movements – where black communities formed their own councils and tried to manage their municipal affairs in a participatory manner.

The ANC also swallowed up the UDF, one of Africa's most effective grass-roots civil movements. The UDF had galvanised a broad range of groups across different classes and races, including black professional organisations and the growing black middle class, who by the 1980s were starting to become sceptical of a 'radical' ANC. It also incorporated liberal white issue-based groups who opposed the apartheid government, such as the End Conscription Campaign.

Compared to other African liberation movements, the ANC had the unique ability to unite diverse groups within South Africa against apartheid. Most other African liberation movements were formed around one ethnic or regional group, and could never transcend this. The ANC created a broad-church alliance that spanned the ideological spectrum, from shopkeepers to communists, and became what was called a 'multi-class' organisation.

The ANC is also one of the few liberation movements that embraced minority communities, including what other liberation movements referred to as 'settlers' (white groups). Joel Netshitenzhe, former editor of the ANC journal *Mayibuye*, once said that 'over the years, the organisation projected itself as a parliament, first, of the African people; and it later sought recognition as the legitimate representative of all the people of SA'. *This* was the strength of the ANC: the ability to portray itself as a more racially inclusive alternative to colonial and apartheid governments.

Three other constituencies – organised women's groups, trade unions and churches – have also been influential in the ANC's long history. In many other African liberation struggles these constituencies may have been present, but were not as prominent as in the ANC.

Of all the African liberation movements, the ANC had the most influential and organised women's wing. Yet, when the ANC was formed it did not accept women as members.

In 1918 when the white-controlled government of the Union of South Africa threatened to introduce pass laws for black women, the ANC was going through one of its most vulnerable periods. Supporters and members of the party were disillusioned with the leadership's ineffectual strategy of petitioning the Union government and the British monarch to give concessions to the oppressed black majority. The militancy of black female activists and their strategy of mass protests against the pass laws filled the conservative ANC male leadership with awe.

The Bantu Women's League was formed in 1918, and joined as a branch of the ANC. It was later succeeded, in 1948, by the ANC Women's League (the ANC first accepted female members in 1943). Women activists also played a part in the penning of the Freedom Charter of 1955.

The ANC has had an extraordinary number of capable churchmen – or lay clergymen – who cut their organisational teeth within the church, but became brilliant mass campaigners. James Calata, who was refused the bishopric of Transkei because he was black, stands out. During one of the ANC's most lethargic periods just before the Second World War, when its finances were in a mess, James Calata was elected general secretary of the ANC. He set up new branches, re-energised dormant ones and balanced the books.

The ANC's alliance with trade unions not only brought the trade-union emphasis on internal democracy, broad consultation and sensitivity to bread-and-butter issues, but also boosted the organisation at critical moments when it seemed to lose direction. The ANC's alliance with the SACP bought funding, resources and training for ANC members from the SACP's main backer, the Soviet Union, and brought dedicated strategic thinkers, such as Joe Slovo, into the ANC.

Unfortunately, as the ANC celebrates its centenary, antidemocratic leaders and groups seem to have a stranglehold on the party. Members are deeply divided over the spoils of government and its current leader Zuma is being accused of using state resources to enrich his family, friends and political allies.

Key ANC leaders wrote South Africa's post-apartheid Constitution, which set out a clear framework for a new South Africa. Globally it is accepted as among the most progressive, but the ANC appears to find it very difficult to internalise its democratic value system and apply it to its own day-to-day practices. The intelligence and security forces, as well as the police, are routinely used in ANC leadership battles. Corrupt officials appear to be selectively prosecuted as part of campaigns to sideline opponents. One fears that these cloak-and-dagger-style operations are a sign that rogue elements within the ANC's military and intelligence wings have now become dominant.

Control of the leadership of the ANC has now become a no-holds-barred war between different factions. Winning office increasingly translates into control of state patronage and the ability to put oneself above the law. Or, at least, some ANC leaders seem to think this way.

The contrast between the moral authority of a Nelson Mandela, an Oliver Tambo or an Albert Luthuli, and the murkiness of a Jacob Zuma, who is seeking re-election as party leader this year, shows how far the ANC has regressed. In his 2007 campaign to become leader of the ANC many Zuma supporters went '100% Zulu' in their support for the man from KwaZulu-Natal – out of the window went the inclusive ethos of the ANC of old.

The DA is currently appealing to the Supreme Court of Appeal to have corruption charges against Zuma, which were dropped in 2009 on a technicality, revisited. If successful, Zuma, a standing president, may have to reappear in the dock.[1]

In the midst of the grinding poverty endured by the ANC's bedrock constituency, levels of corruption, wastage of public resources and conspicuous consumption by elected officials have rocketed. The ANC in government appears to have made the mistake that all the failed African liberation movements have made – enriching the few, mostly those who are politically connected, rather than the poverty-stricken masses.

Increasingly, top leaders in the ANC are chosen by small cliques – and at lower levels on slates attached to the top leaders. Leaders are elected not on their holistic leadership merit, but for how best they can balance factional and patronage interests. This means that the most dynamic leaders are unlikely to reach the top.

Blade Nzimande, the general secretary of the SACP, and a close

---

1. In March 2012 the Supreme Court of Appeal (SCA) ruled that the DA must be given access to the records that led to the suspension of criminal charges against Zuma. The National Prosecuting Authority was ordered to make available the record of decision it used when then acting national director of public prosecutions, Mokotedi Mpshe, decided to drop the charges. The SCA judgement also affirmed that a decision to discontinue a prosecution was reviewable by the courts. Helen Zille, the leader of the DA, said: 'The record of decision will shed light on whether Mokotedi Mpshe made the decision to withdraw the prosecution on rational, legal grounds, or whether he made the decision based on political considerations.'

ally of Zuma, has said publically that leaders of the ANC, COSATU and his SACP are now regularly using money to buy votes in internal ANC elections. 'It is blood money, often gotten corruptly. They go around buying delegates. If those people can capture our government they will sell this country to the highest bidder,' said Nzimande.

COSATU General Secretary Zwelinzima Vavi has warned: 'If we do not do something about corruption we will find ourselves in a predatory state, where the social order of feeding will be as it is alleged in Angola and Kenya.' This was after a multibillion-rand Arcelor-Mittal deal in which family members and friends of President Jacob Zuma controversially received valuable shares in the Sishen mine. In such a predatory state, Vavi said, 'the first family becomes the first to feed, followed by the cabinet and provincial leadership, and our people come last to find absolutely nothing – not even bones'.

In the past, genuinely democratic leaders have sprung up from within or come from outside to move the ANC back onto the right path. Recently, a number of new civil groups have been formed to try and do just this. Corruption Watch, launched last year by trade unions and civil groups, and the Council for the Advancement of the South African Constitution (CASAC), launched by such luminaries as the former speaker of parliament Frene Ginwala, are examples of two such organisations. But unless truly democratic groups take control of the ANC, and elect a better calibre of leaders, the ANC may lose its way completely.

ARISE magazine, March/April 2012

Zuma: An indebted president

Hard work lies ahead for Zuma

The mandate given to South Africa's ruling African National Congress (ANC) (just short of two thirds of the vote) in last week's elections is a poisoned chalice. It is clear that the election of Jacob Zuma as ANC leader in 2007 has energised South Africa's electorate. Voter turnout was more than 70% in this election.

Some white South Africans, who seemingly gave up on politics after the loss of political power in 1994, have returned. Many appear to have voted to prevent Zuma's ascendancy, by casting their ballot for the traditionally white Democratic Alliance (DA) or the Congress of the People (COPE), the party formed by ANC dissidents last year. Many middle-class black people, also opposed to Zuma, have broken their allegiance to the ANC and voted for COPE.

But poor blacks, who had drifted away because of the party's patchy delivery record, have returned to vote for the ANC, persuaded by Zuma's promises. Party leaders have successfully presented themselves as a new ANC that will be pro-poor, more accountable and less corrupt – blaming government failures on the leadership of the outgoing president, Thabo Mbeki.

Sadly, the election campaign brought few details of how the promises made were to be delivered. Zuma's challenges are formidable: improving public services, assembling competent staff – which means not purging senior civil servants critical of him – tackling corruption and restoring the credibility of democratic institutions.

Desperate black voters, who gave the ANC this victory, did so in a last-ditch hope that its leaders will turn their promises into action. That calls for Zuma to roll up his sleeves from Day One. He is unlikely to have the honeymoon period that previous ANC governments had. If the ANC does not deliver this time, people are likely to plunge back into apathy or protest strongly, even violently.

Having turned out in their millions, the challenge now is for South Africans to stay politically active. They must hold the new government accountable, to prevent the abuse of power that we have seen in recent years. It is also clear that South Africa has too many opposition parties, with few policy differences. Some of them will do well to merge, or even to become nongovernmental organisations (NGOs).

To capture the presidency, Zuma assembled a disparate coalition and made often conflicting promises to each group. We now face the possibility that disappointment and infighting in the coalition may trigger another fracture within the ANC. In the successful campaign to get the corruption charges against Zuma dropped, democratic institutions were damaged, and their credibility is now in tatters. Zuma must steer clear of appointing uncritical acolytes, and make the ANC internally democratic.

The DA has won in the Western Cape, giving it the opportunity to show it can govern competently and inclusively. Zuma must re-frain from withholding resources from this region. COPE, given that it lacked resources and was only launched last December, did well to capture more than a million votes. These parties now have enough support to hold the ANC more accountable.

South Africa desperately needs a serious party on the left of the political spectrum, with roots in the 'struggle'. The Congress of South African Trade Unions (COSATU) and the South African Communist Party (SACP) had planned to form such a party, but were persuaded to back Zuma. The ANC under Zuma is too broad a coalition to turn into a left-wing party, as some of the trade unionists and socialists backing him hope. Yet dashed expectations and failure to deliver on promises may still trigger a left-wing break within the ANC, and herald a major reconfiguration of party politics.

The Guardian, 26 April 2009

The glue that binds

Jacob Zuma and the ANC ran a brilliant campaign that successfully framed the 2009 election as a face-off between well-off blacks and whites on the one hand and the poor black majority on the other – rather than on an examination of the government's record in power.

Zuma was voted in by the majority of poor black South Africans, for whom little has changed since 1994. To win an election in South Africa the support of the black poor and working class in townships, rural areas and informal settlements, more than 60% of the population, is crucial.

Zuma successfully portrayed himself as 'poor', identifying his personal marginalisation by former president Thabo Mbeki with the marginalisation of the poverty-stricken masses. He successfully distanced himself from the failures of the ANC government in the minds of poor voters, blaming them on Mbeki.

Throughout the election campaign, his strategists portrayed his camp, which now dominates the ANC, as almost a different party altogether. They projected Zuma and the new leadership as more pro-poor and democratic – and paradoxically less corrupt – suggesting they will offer effective government.

Zuma tapped into a dramatic change in the mood of South Africa's poor black majority. Forgotten by the elite, they have run out of patience and are now demanding the economic dividends of democratic rule. Some poorer South Africans blame democracy itself for their marginalisation, rather than government incompetence, leadership indifference and public corruption. For many, the sixteen formidable charges Zuma sidestepped were 'manufactured' by Mbeki and rich blacks and whites who oppose a poor 'peasant' from Nkandla in rural KwaZulu-Natal.

Zuma successfully portrayed the abuse of democratic institutions by the Mbeki administration – of which he was a member until 2005 – as an attempt to exclude a downtrodden peasant and champion of the poor from the presidency and a manifestation of the marginalisation of the dispossessed under democracy. Ominously, such framing creates a climate for political leaders to batter democratic institutions without risking much opposition from ordinary citizens. In their campaign against Zuma's corruption charges, the new ANC leadership closed down the Scorpions without consulting parliament, which should have decided the issue, while repeatedly attacking critical media and judges who ruled against him.

COPE was unable to counter the ANC's message that it forms part of a rich black and white cabal which opposes the interests of the poor. It and the DA focused their campaigns on Zuma's compromised morals and attacks on democratic institutions. This may have resonated with the black and white middle classes, but it fell on stony ground among those living in shacks, without jobs or food, who cling to Zuma's promises of free health care, education and social grants.

One thing is clear: the glue that binds the different factions within the ANC family is not consensus over policies, the direction of the country or ideology, but getting Zuma elected president. To capture the top office, he has assembled a disparate coalition by telling every group exactly what it wants to hear. Often the pledges are contradictory and some of his supporters are heading for disappointment. Dashed expectations and infighting in the coalition over how to address South Africa's urgent problems under a Zuma presidency may trigger another split in the ANC.

And he is unlikely to have the honeymoon period enjoyed by past ANC governments. If he fails to deliver, the poor will also turn against him. His initial response to these pressures is not encouraging. Not yet formally in power, he has copied many vices of the Mbeki era from which he has distanced himself.

To prove his detractors wrong, he must use the best talents of all South Africans from all race groups, whether they are critical of him or not, rather than rewarding incompetent cronies, dodgy financial backers or those from the same ethnic group as himself. He must do more than talk about defending the Constitution, and democratic institutions and values, but reflect such commitments in his behaviour. As Zuma assumes the presidency, he would do well to heed the warning of ANC veteran Mac Maharaj: 'It is actions that are going to inspire confidence.'

Mail & Guardian, 25 April 2009

The fight over Zuma

The fierce battle to oust former president Thabo Mbeki and his allies, at the ANC's seminal December 2007 national conference in Polokwane, brought together an alliance of two broad but diametrically opposed groups. For very different reasons, both groups rallied behind Jacob Zuma in his battle with Mbeki, and so lifted him into the presidency.

The one thing that both groups have in common is that they successfully used the popular discontent among the ANC rank and file and ordinary South Africans to their advantage. At the heart of this discontent was a strong feeling that the leadership, party, government and democratic institutions had become unaccountable, uncaring and unresponsive. Ordinary ANC supporters expected the dividends of democracy – jobs, houses and a crime-free environment – to accrue to them also, not only to a small elite, whether black (associated with the ANC leadership) or white (the apartheid elite), who are doing well in the democratic dispensation.

Within the Zuma coalition, one group saw the wave of discontent among the ANC rank and file as a genuine cry for the ANC and government to become more transparent, accountable and pro-poor. This group wants all the corrupt, unaccountable public representatives to be brought to book, for service delivery to be speeded up and for the ANC itself to be modernised into a more internally democratic organisation. They are the new modernisers and though some were opposed to rallying behind Zuma in the first place, they 'pragmatically' accepted him as a conduit or transition point for the modernisation of the ANC after Polokwane.

The other group within the coalition used the rhetoric of transparency, accountability and pro-poor policies to grab power for personal, factional and ethnic reasons. This group also wants to purge all levels of government of public representatives, not necessarily because of mismanagement or corruption, but to take their place and become rich themselves. They have a very narrow view of democracy, and basically want things to remain the same as under Mbeki. The only change would be that they and their allies are now in charge. This group could be called the opportunists.

Polokwane was not an ideological battle between the left and the right wings of the ANC but between two different factions, and now that Thabo Mbeki and his allies have been overthrown, both the opportunists and the new modernisers are pressing President Zuma for change – often diametrically opposed versions of change.

The crisis of conflicting claims is played out at local level in the current wave of community protests against poor government service delivery. Some people genuinely want change at the local level – they want corrupt local councillors, local ANC leaders and indifferent public servants to be brought to book. Others just want to replace them so that they can have their turn at the trough.

The battle is going on across government. In some instances departmental directors-general, boards and CEOs of parastatals and democratic institutions are under pressure. Again, some genuinely want to bring new accountability to institutions by appointing a better calibre of person. Yet others only want themselves and their friends in the pound seats.

The extraordinary early discussions among some sections of the ANC, which revolved around replacing the top six ANC leaders, including General Secretary Gwede Mantashe – or re-electing them in 2012, even though the new government has hardly found its feet – are a manifestation of the battle for supremacy between the opportunists and the new modernisers. These two groups stood uncomfortably next to each other in the trenches in their fight against Mbeki. Now that Mbeki is gone, the glue that held them together has come unstuck.

How Zuma will walk the tightrope between these opposing groups within his coalition will define his legacy. Taking the side of the genuine democrats in every coming conflict will be politically risky for Zuma – it could mean unravelling his coalition and creating new enemies, who will turn against him. Furthermore, in the most extreme scenario, this battle between the new modernisers and the opportunists, unless creatively resolved, may actually split the ANC again.

Zuma strategists may calculate that the safest solution would be to please every group just enough – to on occasion give concessions to one group; and on other occasions, to the other. This will mean that the cause of democracy will in some instances be boosted, and in other instances be undermined. It will be a case of one step forward, and then one step back.

This will also mean that the Zuma coalition remains together in an uncomfortable embrace. The outcome of this compromise scenario may mean muddled policies to please both sides and the danger is that the battle between these opposing groups – opportunists and new modernisers – could keep government in paralysis and Zuma's presidency in a continual log jam.

But in the long term, neither the ANC nor the country can afford muddling along. This moment calls for clear vision at the centre, decisive leadership and democratisation of party and government.

The better response, in terms of long-term consolidation of democracy within the ANC and the country, is for Zuma to take the side of democracy at each and every internal conflict of the ANC. This will bring genuine democracy to the ANC and the country. At the same time it will create formidable enemies for Zuma, and may lead to him completing only a single term, or even less, in government. Yet this strategy will seal Zuma's legacy as a democrat, and rescue the ANC's democratic legacy.

Sowetan, 24 September 2009

The truth about keeping broad coalitions together

This month has been something of a watershed for COSATU and the SACP: they have come to realise that though they may have carried Zuma into the South African presidency, this does not mean that they will dominate policy in the post-Polokwane era.

The analysis from strategists in both COSATU and the SACP is now that they may have to compete with other lobbies – such as the nationalist-populist wing, personified by the ANC Youth League, and the powerful black business wing of the ANC – for Zuma's ear.

Although sidelined under Mbeki, the SACP and COSATU would have expected that under the new president they would give the ideological, intellectual and strategic direction to the ANC government.

The truth is, historical examples elsewhere in the developing world show that, when in government, it is very difficult to hold together such an ideologically divergent coalition, consisting of nationalists, traditionalists, populists, business figures, communists and social democrats. An alliance as broad as the one Zuma is currently trying to hold together can almost only be maintained when fighting a discredited colonial, minority or even military regime. In government, it can most probably only work if every group signs a mutually agreed pact, in which the core policies, service delivery time frames, leadership quotas for each group and transparent rules to hold them accountable are clearly spelled out.

The current realignment within the ANC family is a direct result of the storm unleashed at Polokwane – where the leadership baton was passed from Mbeki to Zuma (an action which led to the formation of COPE by centrist supporters of Mbeki who were angry at his brutal dismissal). The grouping of ANC centrists who have not left for COPE are now in retreat. They are scattered, no longer a coherent force, and some of them have even been co-opted by Zuma – understandable when you consider that their political survival, in one way or another, is now dependent on his largesse.

Included in the realignment within the ANC family is the planned formation next year of a 'party of the left', by members of the SACP and COSATU who opposed the two organisations' support for Zuma at the Polokwane conference. This group, mostly provincial leaders of the two formations, is planning a conference in March next year to lay the foundations of a new 'democratic' leftist party. They insist that Zuma's credentials fall well short, and therefore he cannot be supported by the ANC left as a candidate for the presidency of the ANC and the country. Many of those who argued this were purged by SACP and COSATU leaders. Sidelined, they want to marshal communities protesting spontaneously across the country against poor local government service delivery, corruption and inefficiency behind their cause.

They also want to mop up disgruntled members of other group-ings on the black left – the remaining supporters of the rapidly dis-integrating Pan Africanist Congress of Azania (PAC), and those of the increasingly flat-footed Black Consciousness parties, such as the Azanian People's Organisation (AZAPO) and the Socialist Party. They are also wooing the grass-roots movements that broke away from the ANC after the 2000 local government elections, such as the Anti-Privatisation Forum, Abahlali baseMjondolo, a shackdwellers' movement, and the Western Cape Anti-Eviction Campaign, which are often labelled within the ANC left as 'ultra-left'.

Where will all of this end? Possibly, this infighting within the Zuma-ANC coalition could go on until the ANC's 2012 national con-ference. This will mean, of course, that there will be paralysis in both the ANC and government until then. Delivery cannot happen when there is paralysis at the centre of government and the ruling party. Yet, if the pace of delivery slows still further and is combined with public infighting among ANC leaders and conspicuous consump-tion – amidst rising poverty and unemployment among the black majority – more and more ordinary ANC supporters will think of deserting the party. This is especially true if credible alternative political parties start to form outside the ANC.

In this scenario, the ANC's 2012 national conference could turn into a battle between – and within – the left (COSATU and the SACP) and the assortment of nationalists, populists, traditionalists and business figures that occupy the centre and centre-right. Such a fight won't be about policies or ideology, but over personalities, leadership positions and control of the state.

Out of this potentially bloody tussle, no one group among the SACP and COSATU or the different nationalist-populist-traditionalist permutations (whether with the support of key black business figures or not) will emerge victorious. In the aftermath, the losing factions have a choice – to compromise or keep fighting from the margins, and thus sustain the cycle of government paralysis. Of course, the SACP and COSATU could walk out and form a 'workers' party' – if they lose the 2012 battle. And, however unlikely, there is still always a chance that the infighting could splinter the ANC into a number of smaller components – with a new group of parties arising from the ashes.

Sowetan, 17 December 2009

Does Zuma have what it takes?

Jacob Zuma and his supporters were very annoyed when critics persistently asked whether their hero has the character and moral fibre to rally a divided ANC and anxious South Africa behind him. Earlier this month, Archbishop Emeritus Desmond Tutu called on Zuma to drop out of the ANC leadership race, citing his irresponsibility in having unprotected sex and his supporters' hostile attitude towards his alleged rape victim.

In politics character does matter, especially if one competes for the top leadership position of a party and government. In the dizzying campaign ahead of elections, politicians routinely make contradictory promises. For example, Zuma promised the business sector that he will stay the course of the centrist economic path steered by Mbeki, but he also gave the impression to COSATU stalwarts that he supports more radical redistribution to the poor. Polly Toynbee, the British commentator, argues that it is not frivolous journalism to 'emphasise the nature of the man'. No one can accurately say what leaders really stand for, or predict what they will do once in power.

As Tutu points out, South Africans have lost their idealism. Politicians have also lost the respect of the public, since very few of them appear to have a social conscience or believe in anything bigger than their own enrichment. The idea that civil servants and politicians are there to serve is a fading dream. Moreover, after more than a decade in power, the ANC government and leadership are in serious paralysis and in desperate need of renewal.

South African society itself is crisis. The ideals of the ANC and like-minded progressives – white and black – of creating a good society seem to be collapsing. Our quest is the same as that set out by the Canadian economist JK Galbraith in his book *The Good Society: The Humane Agenda*. In it he calls for an equitable society that shows compassion for the poor while providing economic opportunity for all its citizens. In his Steve Biko lecture at the University of Cape Town, Tutu warned that South Africa was losing its moral direction with children being raped, families breaking down, violent crime, increasing ethnic and racial divisions, and a declining sense of social justice.

There is a deep leadership void at the centre of South African politics. There appears to be no moral purpose at the heart of government, no direction for how to bring new energy to the centre. The opposition parties do not offer much substance either. Any new ANC leader must be able to give a new sense of purpose and energy to the administration. His leadership style should be fresh and more inclusive.

The question remains: Aside from struggle credentials, does Zuma have the required leadership qualities to counter-balance his human failings? Does he have the character and can he convince others to trust him that he will lead South Africa to a brighter future in a world that is in flux? Can he be a catalyst and help to liberate the enormous individual and collective talent of the South African people? Is he someone who can think out of the box and lead us to a point where we can compete with emerging economies, such as China and India?

At this point we do not have the answers to these questions. We can only fall back on past actions and proclaimed principles to assess this presidential candidate's potential for when he assumes power.

The Witness, 27 September 2006

Shift Zuma aside or suffer the consequences

When South Africa's ANC members, supporters and sympathisers voted for Jacob Zuma as leader of the ANC – and later of the country – they knew his private life and personal finances were shambolic. Despite this, at the party's Polokwane national conference in 2007 many rank-and-file members voted for Zuma because they believed that only he could unseat – and had the daring to stand against – former ANC leader Thabo Mbeki.

Following this, in the 2009 national elections, many ordinary South Africans argued that they voted for the ANC as a liberation movement rather than for Zuma the individual. Zuma had promised that under his leadership the ANC 'collective' would deliver jobs, efficient public services and a quality democracy, and they argued that his flawed judgement in his private life did not really matter as long as the government he led kept its promises to the poor. The argument went that Zuma, although an ANC leader, would submit himself as 'a loyal cadre' to the collective values, traditions and policies of the 'movement'. Clearly, the reality is not so straightforward.

The inherent danger of electing someone with such a colourful private life is that sooner or later the excesses of his private life will so dominate public life that they paralyse government itself. This moment has arrived. The floodgates have been opened. It will be difficult to close them now.

The recent 'babygate' revelations have overshadowed everything else and it is unlikely that minds across the country will be concentrated on his state of the nation address on 11 February, in which he will set out the government's priorities for the year. The pattern has been set. Every new revelation that might emerge from his private life will dominate the headlines and public debate. It will distract from his public office.

In such circumstances effective governing cannot take place. Valuable public resources, time and energy – which should be concentrated on the delivery of public services – will be spent on dousing the fires springing from his private life. The tumultuous private life of Zuma the 'individual' may now tarnish the credibility of the collective ANC movement and government also. This is clearly contrary to those who think that Zuma's 'individual' private conduct will be subsumed by the 'collective'. It is in fact the other way round.

ANC members who voted for Zuma on the basis that he would bring effective government are now starting to worry that his private conduct may be such that it will undermine effective government throughout his term. Some far-sighted ANC leaders are waking up to this – this is why Zuma was persuaded to apologise even after the party's spin doctors had insisted that his private sex life had nothing to do with his public life. Public disgust over Zuma's private life might easily translate into rejection of the ANC.

The ANC leadership must soberly consider whether it is not better to get a new leader now, while it is still early days – let Zuma retain the ANC presidency, but move someone else into the nation's presidency – or suffer the electoral consequences.

Sowetan, 11 February 2010

Searching for the soul of the ANC

President Jacob Zuma has carefully chosen his State of the Nation address to coincide with the day that Nelson Mandela was released by the white-minority government after 27 years in prison. His strategy appears to be to show the continuity of the present ANC with that of Mandela's generation. It will do the opposite.

The contrast between the moral authority of Mandela and the

murkiness of Zuma, the current ANC and South African leader, could not be more striking. It is also a powerful indictment of the backsliding of the ANC. Zuma's speech will be overshadowed by the 'babygate' revelations of the out-of-wedlock birth of his four-month-old baby with Sonono Khoza, the daughter of football tycoon Irvin Khoza.

The excesses of the president's private life are now beginning to dominate his public life to such an extent that they may paralyse government for most of his presidential term.

Winnie Madikizela-Mandela, the former wife of Nelson Mandela, last month said the Mandela family was 'sort of keeping him (Nelson Mandela) away from' the daily news of the bickering, scandals and moral indiscretions of the ANC. Madikizela-Mandela said that if her frail ex-husband knew what was happening to the ANC he spent 27 years in jail for, it would 'quicken our journey to eternity'. Of course, Madikizela-Mandela is far from blameless.

During the struggle for liberation, members, activists and supporters of the ANC did not see the movement as simply another ordinary political party. It was supposed to have a soul.

The soul of the ANC was, of course, not easy to define. Yet it was roughly understood that what made the ANC stand apart was its genuine commitment to internal democracy, accountability, honesty and its compelling vision of a caring, nonracial society and governing in the broadest public interest.

When Mandela was released on 11 February 1990, to assume the de facto leadership of the ANC, we naively thought that the ANC would be different. The ANC in government was going to break from the familiar path of African liberation movements having their souls corrupted in power. And in some ways it has – managing, initially, to cobble together a Constitution which set out a post-liberation ideological blueprint of a caring and inclusive society (something which no other post-liberation African country came close to).

Yet what cannot be doubted any more is that our worst fears have come true: the ANC has lost its soul. The question now is whether the party can recapture it – and turn it to the democratic path many dreamed was possible when Mandela walked out of Victor Verster prison twenty years ago. Many have already given up trying. The only way to do so is to overhaul the ANC, root and branch, and turn it into a wholly democratic organisation.

If the ANC's democratic soul cannot be recaptured, it may be better for South African society for the ANC to break up and for new parties to be formed from its ashes.

The Guardian, 11 February 2010

No way to run a democracy

No matter what the ANC's leaders say, the decision to drop corruption charges against the president of South Africa's ruling ANC, Jacob Zuma, is no cause for celebration. It should rather be mourned as a setback for efforts to entrench the rule of law in South Africa's infant democracy.

Zuma was facing sixteen charges, including racketeering, money laundering, corruption and fraud, linked to the controversial multibillion-rand government arms deal. South Africa's National Prosecuting Authority (NPA) simply wilted under pressure from Zuma supporters in charge of the ANC to drop the case before national elections – scheduled for 22 April – in which Zuma will stand as an ANC presidential candidate.

The NPA said it reached its verdict based on possible political interference in the trial. It said it came to the decision after reviewing transcripts of illegally intercepted telephone calls – presented to the NPA by Zuma's legal representatives – in which the former NPA head Bulelani Ngcuka and former head of the Directorate of Special Operations (DSO, also known as the Scorpions), Leonard McCarthy, allegedly discussed the timing of reinstating the charges against Zuma. The NPA said the intercepted telephone records, including those of former president Thabo Mbeki, showed the discussions took place before the ANC national conference in December 2007, where Zuma was elected the new leader of the ANC.

It would have been better if the Zuma case had not been dropped and instead those accused of interference had been investigated and charged alongside him. The same goes for those who illegally tapped telephones. Zuma supporters have depicted his prosecution as part of a conspiracy from within the ANC to prevent him from becoming the president of South Africa. Yet they have been silent on the very real allegations of wrongdoing against him. Zuma's legal representatives have not tried to show that their man is innocent of the corruption charges. Incredibly, they have argued that other ANC leaders have been more corrupt than their man, yet have not been prosecuted, and therefore to charge Zuma would be wrong. He has also threatened to implicate other ANC leaders if he is convicted – a threat that itself should have been probed by the NPA.

Zuma, who could hire the best legal brains available (paid for by the state), has used every loophole to stay out of court, rather than trying to clear his name. Taking on the man who is now the most powerful figure in the ANC was never going to be easy. That is why Bulelani Ngcuka, the former head of the NPA, said in 2002 that although it had prima-facie evidence against Zuma, the authority wouldn't directly take him on, because the political forces ranged in support of the ANC leader were just too powerful. A better strategy, Ngcuka argued, was to go for Zuma's lesser lieutenants: chiefly Schabir Shaik, his former financial advisor – who was eventually successfully prosecuted for corruption.

Yet the NPA has shot itself in the foot by getting the basics wrong and twice letting Zuma off the hook on procedural grounds. Just as instructive is the fact that the ANC leadership cannot see something wrong in having the compromised Zuma – a sexist, populist and social conservative – as presidential candidate. This is in itself an indictment of the ANC's moral backsliding. The Zuma case was not only an example of the manipulation of public opinion by political leaders, it was also a terrible case of idol worship. Perfectly rational people from across the ideological spectrum appear to be unable to ask difficult questions about Zuma's policy agenda. Acting National Director of Public Prosecutions Mokotedi Mpshe said that the 'legal process' in the Zuma case was 'tainted', but the corruption charges remain solid. Yet senior ANC leaders seem blind to this argument. The party treasurer, Mathews Phosa, said, 'We have always said Zuma was innocent and today it was the NPA who said it.'

Many grass-roots ANC members have genuinely fallen for such spin. Many more in rural areas, townships and informal settlements, which do not have access to viewpoints showing Zuma as a compromised man, have fallen for the line that the dropping of the corruption charges against Zuma means that he is 'innocent'. Other ANC supporters who may have a problem with Zuma will nevertheless vote for the ANC based on its liberation record.

Many public intellectuals have argued that a Zuma presidency is unlikely to be any worse than Thabo Mbeki's autocratic leadership. They claim that Zuma will rule as part of an ANC leadership collective, and thus cannot do much harm. Yet Mbeki was supposedly also ruling as part of a leadership collective – and his spectacular failures were in part responsible for plunging South Africa into this mess.

The Guardian, 6 April 2009

What can be expected of Zuma's second term

The ANC – the African continent's oldest liberation movement – is as divided as it has been in living memory. Central to the divisions is President Jacob Zuma, who appears intent on pushing for a second term.

Zuma's critics say this is to prevent prosecution for his alleged involvement in South Africa's controversial 1999 arms deal. His backers retort that he is unfairly maligned by the media and point to his 'common touch' as the reason for his political survival.

Julius Malema, the controversial president of the ANC Youth League and a thorn in Zuma's side, was suspended from the party last November for bringing the ANC into disrepute, sowing division and undermining the presidency. Malema's suspension opens the path for Zuma to be re-elected as president for a second term, but things are not yet cut and dried – the Youth League leader is appealing his sentence and is planning to take his fight all the way to the ANC's national elective conference in Bloemfontein in December 2012.

Malema and the ANC Youth League are not only actively opposed to Zuma's second-term aspirations, they are also the conduit for others to express their opposition. The ANC's centenary year may be one of its most bumpy, with angry ANC Youth League members rebelling against Malema's treatment, leadership battles between various factions over control of resources (in government and the party) and a likely upsurge in protests from poor communities, disenchanted with sluggish public service delivery.

All this in the midst of rising economic hardships resulting from the global financial crisis.

The real danger will come if Malema can convincingly portray his suspension to the disenchanted, and especially the youth, as an attempt by the president to marginalise a 'spokesperson' of the poor. Ironically, this is a tactic Zuma has used himself – when battling former president Thabo Mbeki, he successfully portrayed his sacking for alleged corruption as being motivated by his pro-poor stance.

In young democracies, such as South Africa's, where democratic institutions are still in their infancy, the example set by political leaders is crucial. Zuma was voted in as ANC president in 2007, at the party's Polokwane conference – this was after he and his supporters went on the offensive, attacking the country's judiciary and media in order to ensure that corruption charges against him were quashed. He replaced Thabo Mbeki after promising he would govern more democratically, but in power Zuma has shown scant regard for South Africa's democratic institutions. For instance, the president is ramming through a controversial information bill – giving the government broad powers to classify almost any information involving a state agency as being in the 'interests of national security' – despite widespread opposition from civil society. With jail terms of up to 25 years, the legislation will penalise whistle-blowers, journalists and activists who possess, disclose or even attempt to uncover protected information, and who refuse to reveal the sources of any classified material. Furthermore, Zuma has advocated the establishment of a media appeals tribunal, which will have the power to sanction journalists for 'misconduct'.

Worryingly, South Africa's parliament has no direct oversight of the presidency, and both Mbeki and now Zuma have opposed efforts to change this. In fact, Zuma sparked furious debate by insisting that the judiciary should not 'interfere' with the executive's 'sole discretion' to decide policy. And, in August 2011, Zuma's close political ally and ANC Secretary-General Gwede Mantashe declared that the courts were acting as if they were the political opposition by 'interfering' with the 'right' of elected officials to make policies and laws.

In addition, South Africa's globally admired Constitution is increasingly talked about by those in the Zuma administration as being either against development or an obstacle to faster public service delivery. In fact, Jimmy Manyi, Zuma's former spokesman, has said that 'it appears the Constitution does not support the transformation agenda in this country'. Manyi cites 'freedom of expression' in the Constitution as an example of 'a problem'.

Throughout his presidency, Zuma has been accused of ensuring his family members and associates benefit from 'mega' government and private sector tenders but, despite the president saying he would welcome a discussion in parliament on this, the ruling party seems reluctant to confront the matter head-on – Max Sisulu, the ANC speaker in South Africa's parliament, rejected a request by the opposition DA for just such a debate in August.

One ANC youth leader has described Zuma's presidential style as that of a traditional African chief, using his office to distribute state patronage to allies, friends and family. COSATU Secretary-General Zwelinzima Vavi says that South Africa is 'slipping into a "predatory state", where a new tier of leaders believe it's their turn to feed'. He adds: 'In the process, we have battles of short-term interests.'

The ANC's leadership succession battle in 2007 saw rival factions make use of state security agencies, the police and intelligence services to try and eliminate rivals. At the height of the tussle, a state of paranoia reigned. Alarmingly, it appears that this is still with us – for instance, the alleged use of illegal phone hacking, according to investigations carried out by the *Mail & Guardian* newspaper.

Zuma comes from the ANC's intelligence wing, the most shadowy, secretive and heavy-handed organ of the party in exile. It is the culture of this body that appears to be dominating the state and the ANC at present. For instance, days after Public Protector Thuli Madonsela found that the then police commissioner, Bheki Cele, a key Zuma ally, had acted improperly in arranging a multimillion-dollar lease for new headquarters from a friend, the police raided her office to search for documents related to the report.

However, Zuma's subsequent cabinet reshuffle, in which he fired two ministers accused of corruption and suspended Cele from his duties, has given the president a much-needed boost. But this does not mean that a second presidential term for Zuma is not going to continue the same trajectory as the first: paralysis in government as he pays back diverse backers, battered democratic institutions and the entrenchment of undemocratic values and behaviour.

The legacy of which may all take a very long time to undo.

BBC Focus on Africa magazine, January/March 2012

Zuma: the pressure is on

Every public action by President Jacob Zuma is now almost solely aimed at securing a second term as president of the ANC and the country – rather than promoting the interests of South Africa Inc.

Zuma's bid for a second term is now the single most divisive issue in the ruling ANC-COSATU-SACP alliance. Most of his former supporters have lost confidence in him – those who genuinely but naively thought he would be effective have been disappointed in his poor leadership and his inability to deliver on his promises, and those who were more cynical, who supported him because they thought he would deliver patronage to them in return, have also been left high and dry. The battle for the leadership of the ANC is now being fought between these two groups and the remaining hardline Zuma loyalists.

In the midst of this, Zuma has made the decision to move on two fronts – backing an arms deal probe and sanctioning the disciplining of ANC Youth League leader Julius Malema for bringing the ANC into disrepute.

Zuma's announcement that he will initiate an inquiry into South Africa's multimillion-rand arms procurement deal was most certainly designed to pre-empt a separate pending judgement which would have compelled a judicial commission to investigate. It is likely that he reckons a presidentially appointed commission gives him more scope to appoint sympathetic investigators and define favourable parameters for the inquiry.

Malema and the ANC Youth League oppose Zuma's re-election. Initially they did so in typical ANC style (in code and indirectly), but now that Zuma has hauled Malema and his cohorts to a disciplinary hearing they openly campaign to unseat him. Significantly, other

77

opponents of Zuma in the ANC have joined the Malema group in their bid. For example, younger presidential hopefuls, who only supported Zuma during his Polokwane battle against former ANC and South African president Thabo Mbeki because he promised to stay on for only one term, are now so outraged that they are prepared to side with the Malema group. This is why the likes of Tokyo Sexwale, the human settlements minister, can be found among the witnesses appearing in support of Malema at his disciplinary hearing.

It is not Zuma's style to take on someone like Malema. His normal modus operandi would be to do nothing until the ANC's 2012 conference and then offer a compromise on nationalisation or the other policy and leadership changes that Malema and the ANC Youth League are demanding (excepting a change in president). It was not really the fact that Malema called for nationalisation and regime change in Botswana that angered Zuma; it was that Malema and the Youth League were so close to unseating him. Furthermore, Zuma's strategists appear to be believe, most probably rightly, that Malema is fronting for more senior ANC leaders (including individuals Zuma believed were close allies) who want to unseat the president.

Zuma's announcement that Police Commissioner Bheki Cele must explain the police leasing-contracts-for-pals saga can be read in the same way – the president appears to have started to take the regular reports that Cele, a close ally, has switched his allegiance to ANC factions opposed to Zuma's second term seriously (Cele has strenuously denied this).

Many ANC leaders oppose the reopening of the arms deal because some of the proceeds financed the ANC's operations. Some also appear to fear Zuma may want to use any inquiry to sideline opponents of his second term before the 2012 ANC conference. This view is strengthened by the fact that it seems that in making his announcement of a coming arms deal inquiry Zuma acted alone, without consulting the ANC's National Executive Committee (NEC) or the cabinet. Similarly, it appears Zuma also acted alone when he decided to institute disciplinary proceedings against Malema. Some ANC NEC leaders (excluding ANC General Secretary Gwede Mantashe, whom Malema and the ANC Youth League want to replace as general secretary) want to have another round of 'discussions' with Malema first.

Malema and the ANC Youth League hope a rising anti-Zuma sentiment within the ANC's NEC will result in the NEC rejecting a harsh verdict – if such a verdict should come from the disciplinary committee. Should Malema for instance be suspended or even expelled and the ANC NEC or the ANC national conference (to be held in December 2012) decide to overturn the decision, it will in reality be a vote of no confidence in Zuma's leadership.[2] This will make it very difficult for the president to stay on beyond 2012. Malema and the Youth League's announcement of a mass mobilisation campaign for 'jobs' later in October is also meant to increase the pressure on Zuma from within the ANC. This, after all, is how Zuma and Malema dislodged Mbeki.

Rapport, 22 September 2011

---

2   On 24 April 2012 the ANC National Disciplinary Committee of Appeal upheld a previous decision by the ANC's National Disciplinary Committee to expel Malema for five years.

Rising poverty, rising crisis

South Africa's success is about 'we', not 'me'

Almost every developing country that has become rich since the Second World War has done so by lifting the majority of people out of poverty collectively. In fact, the developing countries that have been most successful since the Second World War, particularly those from the East Asian developmental states, have done so by empowering the widest number of people – not just an elite. Where only a small elite has become prosperous, the countries have stagnated.

Even the post-Second World War Western European reconstruction was premised on a social contract which was based on lifting everyone out of poverty together, and not only a few lucky ones. In fact, this is the basis of the Western European welfare state – that everyone in society must be looked after, not only the political, economic and cultural elite.

Sadly, it is now clear that since 1994 the economic dividends of South Africa's democracy have only benefited a small elite – the old apartheid-era white establishment, which has now been joined by a small black elite. The overwhelming majority of black South Africans remain trapped in grinding poverty. The gap between rich and poor in South Africa is now so wide that research by Haroon Bhorat, University of Cape Town economics professor, shows that the country has now officially become 'the most unequal society in the world'. This ever-deepening divide between the affluent and the destitute is not only any more just between blacks and whites, but also between a minority of rich blacks and the majority poor blacks.

The tragic story in Africa is that almost every African liberation and independence movement that came to power went on to create a situation where only a small elite benefited from the end of colonialism or white-minority rule. Many of those who got rich after independence and liberation were those who were connected to leaders or dominant factions, families and regional or ethnic groups of the liberation or independence movements. The post-independence elite who have become rich have done so mainly by exploiting their struggle credentials and 'political connectivity', while the overwhelming majority of those less connected, but who have most probably sacrificed more during the struggle, starve.

When only a small elite becomes rich, and that elite also has control of political power, as is the case in South Africa and other post-independence African societies, the issues of the poor are unlikely to be determinedly pushed. National and provincial cabinet ministers, mayors and councillors live in huge mansions in exclusive suburbs, drive R1-million cars and surround themselves with bodyguards. Their electricity, water bills, and children's school fees are subsidised by the state.

To imagine that the new elite will somehow support a basic income grant for every poor family that lives in devastating poverty is just foolish. History shows us that this new black liberation and independence elite retain their legitimacy by either giving patronage to selected groups, or to just enough poor people to prevent widespread social rebellion at the injustice of only a small section of the population benefiting from the fruits of liberation. In every African country the leadership has sustained this disgusting inequality by spouting liberation rhetoric and slogans, and professing in public their 'commitment' to the poor.

These leaders often control the flow of information, so the majority of the movement's members and supporters never hear of their conspicuous consumption. They are also in the habit of deflecting scrutiny by blaming colonialism, imperialists or individuals, parties or organisations linked to the pre-liberation order. Alternatively, the newly rich portray members, activists and supporters who criticise this inequality as somehow opposed to the advancement of the poor. Critics with struggle credentials who cannot be dismissed are muzzled – by the security apparatus, police, intelligence services and tax authorities.

The African independence elite have always seen success not as lifting the widest number of people out of poverty but in terms of how a 'struggle' individual can 'accumulate and display the most wealth'. Those who cannot do so are seen as having 'failed'. Yet, unless we measure success as lifting the greatest possible number of the black majority out of poverty, in the shortest time, we will fail as a country. And we will join the club of developing countries that just muddle along, with a small political and economic elite in charge and a poor majority trapped in poverty, from which a small number occasionally join the ranks of the rich.

Sowetan, 5 November 2009

COSATU and the SACP should heed the warning signals

The conventional wisdom among the Congress of South African Trade Unions (COSATU) and South African Communist Party (SACP) strategists, and many other commentators, in business, civil society and opposition parties, is that exploding poverty should naturally strengthen the power of the left within the tripartite alliance. Yet the reverse may actually hold true. In fact, despite the central role COSATU and the SACP played in the 'Zunami' that swept Jacob Zuma into the Union Buildings and Luthuli House, both these organisations are in real danger of losing so much influence that by the end of the Zuma presidency they may end up as lobby groups within the African National Congress (ANC).

Rising poverty may actually strengthen support for populist, tribalist and narrow nationalist politics, rather than leftist or progressive politics. The costs of severe mass poverty are mass alienation, mass family breakdown and mass breakdown in individual self-esteem – especially in South Africa, where self-worth is now increasingly measured in how much money one has. Mass poverty may also cause mass rejection of democracy as a solution to problems.

In the South African context, in moments of crisis, people often seek solace in tradition, tribe and patriarchy. These frequently are translated into over-assertions of Africanness or blackness, or ethnicity expressed as an overemphasis on 'Zulu-ness' or 'Xhosa-ness' as the main source of identity. Socially, these are deeply conservative sentiments. Yet, at the same time, those alienated because of poverty may readily support radical changes normally associated with 'left' positions.

The reality is that rising poverty in South Africa is changing society and opening up a gaping hole at the centre of the country's politics. Many of the current political parties, social movements and democratic institutions are not attuned to these changes, even if they profess in rhetoric to be so. The spontaneous community protests against lack of government service delivery, corruption and indifferent public officials are a case in point. They caught many organised civil groups and parties by surprise. For instance, the South African National Civic Organisation (SANCO), supposedly an organisation fighting on behalf of local communities, was spectacularly absent. In fact, rapid changes in society, associated with increased poverty and alienation – and the SANCO leadership's inability to respond to this – are partially to blame for the organisation being on the verge of extinction.

Some populist leaders in the ANC with a more developed political antenna have already exploited these changes in society, adopting supposedly leftist positions, such as 'nationalisation', when it comes to economics, but combining this with social conservatism – approving of polygamy and virginity testing – and adopting muscular policies to deal with social problems, such as crime.

For COSATU leaders the dangers should be obvious – job losses reduce their membership base. The poor – the jobless, homeless, rural peasants and the young – are now in electoral terms the overwhelming majority. With a smaller base, the trade union federation will face the danger of becoming a 'labour aristocracy', of organising only a small working-class base that have jobs.

The SACP is organised as an elite movement, with a relatively small membership, typically trade unionists, students and those working in civil society. As more and more South Africans become poorer, the membership of the SACP will become even more unrepresentative of the majority.

Unless the SACP and COSATU dramatically refocus, modernise and change strategic direction their influence may decline, rather than increase. To adapt, COSATU may have to start operating more as a social movement and focus specifically on organising the unemployed, rural poor and youth. It will also have to play a bigger role in agitating for housing, public transport and dealing with crime. This will be new territory.

At the same time the SACP will have to turn itself into a party for the masses, with community, youth and rural branches. A broad-based SACP and a socially active COSATU will not only have to provide answers on economic and political issues, but also progressive answers to the difficult questions of individual alienation, family breakdown, establishing a more caring male identity, how to achieve genuine gender equality and how to find a balance between tradition and democratic values. Unless COSATU and the SACP make the crucial adjustments now they will cede influence to the populists and narrow nationalists in the future.

Sowetan, 7 January 2010

When democracy fails the poor

To blame 'third force' or criminal elements or even closet supporters of former president Thabo Mbeki for the wave of service delivery protests over mismanagement and indifferent local authorities is irresponsible. The true 'third force' behind the community protests that are sweeping the country is poverty.

Under the Mbeki administration, the preferred solution was to blame a 'third force', send in the police in a show of force, dispatch a few agents of the National Intelligence Agency (NIA) , then arrest so-called 'ringleaders'. To repeat the Mbeki approach would not only inflame grass-roots passions further, but it would also be patently hypocritical, when the new administration under President Jacob Zuma came to power precisely because it campaigned to end such strong-arm tactics, and promised to be more pro-poor, pro-democracy and to speed up service delivery.

The reality is also that many ANC leaders during and before the April national elections irresponsibly whipped up expectations of immediate delivery. The protesters are mostly ANC supporters, sympathisers and voters. They are protesting because the democracy has failed them. It is likely that many have already approached local elected representatives over slow service delivery, mismanagement and corruption, and were arrogantly rebuffed. Others have most probably also approached local branch leaders of the ANC to complain, but their complaints have fallen on stony ground. In such circumstances, taking to the streets is often the only option remaining. This situation means that both the democratic institutions within the ANC and within broader society have failed. This must be fixed. It is going to be very difficult for the president to send senior ANC leaders to protesting communities to tell them to be patient – they have been patient for fifteen years now.

It is also likely that any message to protestors that the global financial crisis will make it harder to create jobs, deliver houses and roll out social services faster will be rejected. South Africa is in a recession, true, but leaders are still splashing out, buying cars of R1,5 million and regularly throwing huge parties on taxpayers' money. This has enraged many ordinary citizens. To ask communities to tighten their belts, moral authority is necessary, and conspicuous consumption and extravagant expenses erode the moral authority of leaders.

President Zuma must declare an emergency – as part of a broader package to fight off the devastating effects of the recession – in the twenty most depressed municipalities across the country. He then needs to fire those who prove to be corrupt or incapable of managing, or run patronage machines, especially if these are close political allies. Where possible, national government must take over these municipalities, for a restricted period, until capacity is restored. The president must then call for applications for all vacant jobs – nationally and internationally. He must then personally make it a priority to oversee the appointment of only the best candidates – cutting out political and ethnic patronage appointments. And then let the new appointees sign performance contracts – which should be enforced.

The recession has made it more urgent for the president to roll out a universal basic income grant to the poorest. Then he must ban all ministers from buying expensive cars, as well as banning all official government parties, junkets and lunches.

The promise of Polokwane – the renewal of the ANC's internal democratic processes – must also be made real now. Democratic elections, decision- and policy-making and participation within the ANC, from branch level upwards, must now be enforced. Poorer black South Africans want both the democratic and economic fruits of the post-apartheid dispensation – they deserve it, and it is long overdue.

Sowetan, 30 July 2009

When a government fails its people

The horrific incidents of xenophobia sweeping across greater Johannesburg, which have left at least 22 dead, thousands displaced and countless properties destroyed, have been a long time coming.

In fact, attacks against African foreigners have been happening with such frequency across the country that they have, sadly, almost become an accepted feature of life in some parts of South Africa. This wave of violence, which started in the Johannesburg township of Alexandra, had been preceded by months of persistent attacks by locals on foreign Africans, mostly Somali refugees, in the townships surrounding Cape Town.

The influx of African, Asian and Eastern European refugees in the past decade has been the largest single mass migration, in the shortest period, in modern South Africa's history. Just imagine, since 2000 more than three million Zimbabweans have fled disorder to build a new life in South Africa. Many others, whether economic or political refugees, have streamed into South Africa from Nigeria, Congo, Morocco, Sudan, Rwanda and so on.

Although South Africa is one of the world's most unequal societies, with one affluent section – mostly white, though joined in the past decade by a new black middle and upper class – and another, dirt poor – mostly black – the country remains for most Africans, compared to their own, a pot of gold. For the past decade South Africa, the continent's richest economy, has experienced its biggest uninterrupted boom since the post-war growth spurt that ended in 1971. Economic growth has averaged over 5% in each of the last five years. And Johannesburg, the continent's richest city, nicknamed eGoli, place of gold, has been at the centre of that boom. Yet, for many African foreigners, their dreams of gold have turned into dust.

The sheer brutality and rapid spread of the attacks show how deep-seated local resentment against refugees from poorer neighbouring countries is. The xenophobic attacks in the townships have much to do with competition over resources. The combination of inadequate services, rampant food and fuel inflation and little social welfare has become a toxic cocktail. Locals perceive African refugees as taking jobs, houses and resources away from them.

Furthermore, in the midst of the economic boom, government service delivery to blacks living in poor townships has been desperately inadequate. For years now, violent protests against the government's lack of delivery have been commonplace. And while South Africa's economic growth is going on uninterrupted, those in the townships and rural areas are being left behind.

In Johannesburg, African immigrants eke out a living in the informal sector, selling anything from chips to peanuts. However, more than five million black South Africans are also trying to make a living in this sector. These hand-to-mouth businessmen and -women have not benefited from access to bank finance – they still operate in apartheid-like conditions. They are also not connected to the decision makers in the ANC – the ANC politicians-turned-oligarchs, who have changed political 'connectivity' into financial capital through black economic empowerment, are the government's strategy to quickly create black capitalists, not empowering businessmen and -women from the informal sector. And so they vent their anger on African migrants, thinking that they are taking away their customers and livelihood.

But there is also general anti-foreigner sentiment across all races in South Africa. Take, for example, the debate about whether to import skilled foreigners to the country. Many, white and black, are deeply opposed to South Africa importing scarce skills from abroad, the way Australia does. Yet the country is suffering from a desperate shortage of skills at the top end. There is also a perception among some black professionals that white-run companies appoint Africans from outside South Africa as affirmative action candidates, hoping they will be less critical than locals.

The xenophobia is also institutional. South Africa's home affairs department is notoriously unfriendly to refugees and immigrants and when the police bust a criminal syndicate, they often make much of the foreign element in crime. Refugees are routinely rounded up and dispatched to Lindela, a notorious exit camp in the north of the country, from where they are deported by special train and dumped across the border in Mozambique. Most return again, crossing the Limpopo River, the natural border between South Africa and its northern neighbours, which is infested with man-eating crocodiles.

The South African government has badly mismanaged this crisis. Just as it has denied that there are problems over service delivery – not to mention other blind spots, such as the HIV/Aids pandemic – it has also persistently denied that xenophobia is a problem.

Of course, admitting to the problem of xenophobia is also deeply embarrassing to the government because African solidarity is a pillar of the Mbeki presidency. The government's immediate response is an indication of the level of its denial – it blamed a few individuals for being responsible for the violence and announced it would set up a team of experts to look into how to deal with the problem in the long term. That is fine, but refugees need immediate help. The police are hopelessly overstretched and the army will have to be called in.

The real long-term strategy is for the government to deliver services to South Africa's poor, focus on empowering the five million entrepreneurs in the informal sector and launch a massive public anti-xenophobia education drive.

Unless the service delivery issues are decisively dealt with, the next attacks are not going to be on foreigners alone. They will be on neighbours, perhaps of a different colour or ethnicity or speaking a different language, but who are perceived to be doing better.

The Guardian, 20 May 2008

A battle plan to tackle poverty

To be really effective, South Africa's newly envisaged National Planning Commission must operate like the command centre of a country at war, meticulously planning, not against invaders, but the transformation of the economy, as if the country's future depended on it – which it does. South Africa's extraordinarily high levels of poverty, unemployment and inequality are pegged at levels that were seen in many countries only during the Great Depression, or during or in the immediate aftermath of debilitating wars.

Most successful developing countries since the Second World War, especially the East Asian tigers, have had a central structure, managing economic development around a well-thought-through, long-term development plan. Such central planning units make detailed assessments of the state of the economy, then draw up plans to improve it to specific timelines, closely monitoring these plans to see that implementation remains on schedule and, if not, or if the policies appear to be inappropriate, make suitable interventions early on.

They task individuals with responsibility for every facet of the delivery. They make a point of appointing only the best talent in the country to these central planning institutions. Those who don't deliver are fired immediately.

In many countries these planning structures were set up after governments and society in general realised that their countries were in deep economic crisis and they had to do something drastic to quickly lift them out of the morass. Their task was to create economic growth and thereby spread prosperity to the largest number of people in the shortest possible time, and everything was given to them to make this work possible. In response they marshalled the public services behind a common goal: to secure industrialisation in the quickest possible time, according to clear delivery timelines and targets.

South Africa's public service is politicised, riddled with corruption and inefficiency, and appointing the most competent individual for the job is certainly not the norm. On current form the public service will not be able to deliver a successful developmental state along the lines of those in East Asia, and in setting up a national planning commission of the best brains in the country – and giving them a clear mandate, targets and deliverables, and a long-term development plan to pursue – the government may have to accept that it will have to circumvent the public service, at least in the short term, as it is being transformed into a more efficient and accountable one.

In this regard there are some lessons to be learned from South Africa's 2010 World Cup Local Organising Committee, in terms of pursuing targets and meeting deadlines. The kind of urgency and resolve shown by this body must be mirrored by any new planning commission.

Fighting poverty, unemployment and inequality should be like fighting a war. Every resource and talent within the state should be marshalled to tackle these problems as quickly as possible.

Sowetan, 3 December 2009

Corruption:
a call
to arms

The ANC should clean up its house

The now daily but empty anti-corruption rhetoric from our political leaders could be laughed off if the consequences were not so devastating. We must declare corruption a national emergency and corruption busters must have credibility – it is a farce that those paid to fight corruption are perceived in society to be corrupt themselves.

Any serious campaign to deal with corruption must start by tackling political corruption, which provides the incubating environment for other corruption. As the African National Congress (ANC), as the ruling party of South Africa, dominates society, it follows that behavioural norms within the ANC will also dominate society. Therefore, if the cancer of corruption has started to infuse the values and practices of the ANC, it will spill over into broader society. In such an instance, no amount of corruption busting in broader society will uproot it. Eradicating corruption within the ANC itself is a prerequisite for cleaning up corrupt practices in society.

Joel Netshitenzhe, the outgoing government policy chief, rightly warned in an interview with the *Sunday Times* last Sunday that corrupt practices in the ANC will soon reach a 'tipping point' if not stopped 'with all the power of society and by the ruling party itself'. We have to tackle the widespread perception that one can get away with corruption if connected to the 'right' political faction or the leadership of the ANC.

In fact, the culture of corruption will continue if there is a widespread belief – which there is – that some individuals and groups are 'immune' to prosecution because of their political 'connectivity'. The media is awash with glaring cases of the abuse of public resources and funds, but it appears that not a finger will be lifted by the authorities to prosecute the guilty, because those implicated are perceived to be connected to dominant factions or leaders in the ANC.

In any society there must be a sense that rules are applied fairly – if there is going to be broad buy-in to the rules in question. Different rules should not apply to different people, depending on how close they are to the dominant faction or leadership of the ruling party.

Tackling political corruption within the ANC is likely to be career limiting for any leader, activist or party member involved. Those who do so must prepare themselves to become very unpopular – they risk being marginalised, demoted through 'redeployment' or, in the most extreme cases, ousted completely. And life outside government will not be any easier – in business, government tenders will not be forthcoming, and consequently private companies and other organisations wanting to be in the government's good books will stay away from them.

To stop corruption from preventing the attainment of a better life for the majority of South Africans a lot of courageous people are needed both within the ANC and in wider society, not only to support honest corruption fighters, but also to become corruption fighters themselves.

Sowetan, 29 October 2009

Take a critical look at our new heroes

Our new democracy was supposed to usher in a fresh sense of moral responsibility, a new set of social norms and better behaviour. However, today we see an alarming incidence of outrageous public and private impropriety all around us. It is inevitable that some members of any society will try to cut corners or resort to dishonourable means to achieve a specific goal, but it does appear as if there is a weakening of the structures that usually hold the greedy in check.

Conditions in our infant democracy encourage corruption. Firstly, there is the fast-growing gap between the rich and the poor that cannot be justified on individual merit, performance or effort. Related to this are the extraordinarily huge salaries and bonuses that private and public company executives – both black and white – pay themselves each year, even when their performance has been mediocre at best. Often the financial returns for small risk, or none whatsoever, lousy effort and routine duty are just mind-boggling. Will Hutton, author of *The World We're In*, says 'when individuals of only modest talent make extraordinary fortunes for no worthwhile purpose, the consequent impact on the environment in which they operate is devastating.'

99

Few of these payouts can be justified on the basis of sterling effort or performance. Philip Augar, the author of *The Greed Merchants*, explains how very few of the funds managed by investment bankers on Wall Street and in the City of London outperform the average.

Similarly, black professionals are often paid extraordinary wages for their skills, and many are prepared to jump from one job to another just to secure a small salary increase. Not only do their companies lose out, but the larger economy suffers as well, as managers do not acquire the necessary skills to progress in their careers. This situation also leads to subordinate employees thinking that they receive too little in comparison to their bosses. Not surprisingly, they believe that they too deserve the good life that their bosses enjoy.

The ANC's policy of pushing for the rapid expansion of the black middle class (which is not necessarily wrong) and black tycoons (which is wrong) have conversely led to a cult celebration of crass individualism and conspicuous consumption. Now business leaders who have become instantly mega-rich through their political connections in the ANC are black society's new heroes, rather than enterpreneurs who have built up their businesses through hard work and ingenuity.

In addition, our public culture does not encourage a sense of shame in relation to dishonesty. Instead, it celebrates wealth, status and celebrity. On television and in advertising a 'get-rich-quick' mentality is also promoted. Ordinary citizens believe that instant happiness and bliss is around the corner, if only they could win the Lotto or an Idols competition.

The ideal of shared community values – among both blacks and whites – is rapidly unravelling. Even respected institutions, such as churches, succumb to corruption. Politicians and political parties have long since lost their credibility. This is the challenge for our political leaders ahead of the local elections.

Sunday Independent, 19 January 2006

South Africa's 'bling' culture is a disgrace

The socialite Khanyi Mbau, notorious for partying, fast cars and rich 'sugar daddies', is not an oddball. She represents the 'bling' culture which has now become a part of the new South Africa – even our political leadership has become a 'bling' leadership.

There is no difference really between Mbau's actions and those of our political, business and public administration elite. The goal is to get rich quickly, using short cuts (attaching oneself to a sugar daddy, or, in politics, to the boss of a political party), and then, once one has made it, to live lavishly.

The more unfortunate, who do not have the connections or looks, try their luck by addictively playing the Lotto. They dream that one lucky draw will bring fabulous wealth. Others resort to crime to reach their dream of 'bling'. Nobody needs to work or study hard any more; everyone is looking for a short cut.

Black economic empowerment (BEE) has also helped along this 'bling' culture. The downside of BEE as it is practised now is that one does not need to build a business from scratch – which demands entrepreneurial acumen. One can secure a tender through political connections, even if one does not have a clue about how to deliver the services in question.

The unintended consequences of the ANC's policy of deployment also help along this 'bling' culture. By cosying up to the local ANC leadership one can secure a lucrative 'deployment', a ticket to the 'bling' lifestyle. Praise-singing the leadership even if they are wrong, supporting actions that clearly go against prudent values and self-censorship has now became the norm.

Throwing lavish parties at exclusive venues, driving luxury cars worth more than R1 million, wearing R250 000 watches and clothes worth as much as ordinary people would pay for a car – this is the 'bling' lifestyle. Blue-light brigades, huge entourages and being treated as a VIP; ministers going on meaningless foreign junkets and living in expensive hotels; the bonuses, perks and dizzy salaries state-owned companies pay their executives – all of this is part of this 'bling' culture.

The consequences of this 'bling' lifestyle – for the state and South African society in general – are devastating. Scarce resources are being plundered. State capacity is being eroded, which means the ability to deliver basic services is declining. There is no room for entrepreneurship, innovation and new ideas – which are absolutely necessary for economic prosperity.

This 'bling' culture will break down South Africa's productive capacity. We are 'eating', but we are not building any new factories or plants that can create jobs. In the midst of grinding poverty, this 'bling' culture is a disgrace. It encourages corruption and dishonesty, and builds a society based mostly on relationships of patronage – talent, skills and hard work are no longer valued. It corrupts our souls. In fact, it undermines all the values that underpinned the struggle for liberation.

As a society we are losing our bearings. We are on a downward spiral. No caring society was built on 'bling'. Only ridding ourselves of this destructive culture can put our country back on a winning track. We need a new kind of leadership – one that comes without 'bling'.

Sowetan, 4 February 2010

Public servants: stop ducking and diving

When was the last time you heard of a politician or civil servant resigning after being implicated in some impropriety? Accepting personal responsibility for errant behaviour, let alone resigning because of it, is an alien concept to South African politicians and civil servants.

Perhaps the manual on how to respond when you know you are responsible for a misdeed goes along the lines of: stick it out, duck and dive, claim your innocence until the end. If questions still persist, blame the media, a 'third force' or shadowy individuals 'opposed to transformation'. If all else fails, there has to be a nasty racist somewhere who could be responsible.

There appears to be an 'anything goes' spirit among public officials. They seem to brazenly push the envelope of acceptable behaviour and ethical conduct as if knowing that they can get away with it because of their station.

Clearly, ours is not a culture of taking responsibility for wrongdoing. Many would rather have their reputation torn to shreds in public investigations than resign voluntarily. For a case in point, take Jacob Zuma. Before his sacking by President Thabo Mbeki he was given a glut of chances to step down voluntarily. But no, he stuck it out, until he was forced from office. Perhaps if he had stepped down voluntarily, over the initial revelations of his shady links with Schabir Shaik, his integrity and reputation might still have been in place – South Africans have a history of forgiving the openly contrite.

The Zuma situation is replicated everywhere. Visitors to government departments complain on a daily basis about shoddy treatment by petty officials – notices with a telephone number for reporting indifferent or corrupt officials are often to be found on the walls of the office of the official in question – but it is rare that this results in a resignation, or even a change of behaviour for that matter, let alone a sacking.

Power seems to make officials and politicians think they can get away with anything or that they are 'entitled' to certain things because of their station. It appears that they think that they own public institutions, rather than having a duty to the people who elected them.

Being able to hold elected ministers and government officials to account is a pillar of democracy. Without it, the public lose their respect for and confidence in public officials and institutions. Trust breaks down and people begin to take the law into their own hands out of frustration over the lack of accountability, like the man at the Johannesburg home affairs department this week, who held an official hostage – he had been waiting for an ID document for four years.

Sunday Independent, 4 December 2005

Chequebook politics

It appears that a thick wallet increasingly buys one easy access to government leaders, contracts and favourable policies. Last April the ANC set up what it called a 'progressive business forum', which charges businessmen and -women between R3 000 and R60 000 to get face time with ANC leaders and public servants. Sadly, for those who expected better from the ANC, senior members of the party have actually been annoyed by criticism of this controversial scheme – maintaining that there is no reason for anyone to be anxious that it could plunge South Africa further into the quicksand of chequebook politics.

ANC National Spokesperson Smuts Ngonyama insisted the forum provides businessmen and -women with 'regular information on ANC policies and programmes that would be of relevance to them, and interaction with ANC leaders in various forums'.

If this is really the case, why put such a high premium on membership?

Furthermore, Ngonyama says the forum 'promotes honest and productive two-way dialogue between the business community and the ANC'.

This scarcely sounds convincing. During a question-and-answer session at the launch of the business forum in Johannesburg last April, many of the businessmen and -women who had paid to become members told the keynote speaker, Deputy Trade and Industry Minister Rob Davies, that they found it difficult to secure government tenders. Meaning they hoped that now they had become members of this exclusive ANC club they would be able to scoop up government contracts by the bucketful.

Meanwhile, many ordinary card-carrying ANC members at

105

branch level say they have no say in decision- and policy-making and rarely get face-to-face time with their elected representatives. This was one of the main reasons for the grass-roots rebellion against President Thabo Mbeki and the ANC leadership at the movement's seminal June 2005 National General Council. These days, rich individuals whether black or white, big corporates and even parastatals donate large amounts of money to the ANC. Their donations dwarf the amounts received in membership fees, especially since membership has been in decline, as ANC General Secretary Kgalema Motlanthe regularly reports in his annual reports to the party's leadership.

This naturally puts the ANC in a difficult position. If an individual or organisation regularly pays large sums towards the upkeep of the ANC it should not be surprising if the ANC leadership are keen to hear their views. But while BEE tycoons have easy access to senior government officials to complain about not getting government contracts, and their white counterparts to ask for even more favourable laws, the poor are often ignored by public servants and politicians when they complain about pressing poverty, unemployment, homelessness and local crime. Even ordinary ANC members struggle to meet with their local representatives as many claim arrogantly that they have more pressing issues to attend to. And when those without the money to buy an appointment do protest, as they are doing in the spontaneous community protests mushrooming across the country today, government leaders, such as Intelligence Minister Ronnie Kasrils, blame *agents provocateurs* and launch intelligence investigations to fish them out.

The civil groups rightly demanding for government to honour its reparations' obligations for human rights abuses committed by the apartheid state, as recommended by the Truth and Reconciliation

Commission, wait years for hasty meetings with uninterested government officials. The Treatment Action Campaign could only secure face time with Health Minister Manto Tshabalala-Msimang at public meetings – which they often had to gate-crash. COSATU leaders, at one point, could not find an open slot in President Thabo Mbeki's diary for close to eighteen months.

The 'progressive business forum' did not fall out of the sky. It was part of a raft of proposals termed 'modernisation' reforms by senior ANC leaders. A host of these modernisation proposals were rejected by grass-roots members at the ANC's June 2005 national policy conference. Some of them were then taken up by the ANC's National Executive Committee (NEC) for further debate. Others have been referred to the ANC's national conference, to be held in December 2007. One of these is a proposal to give business members special voting powers at ANC gatherings. If this is accepted, it will be the end of the idea of equality of membership the ANC has always professed fealty to. In fact, it will entrench the perception that those with bulging bank balances are more equal than their poorer comrades.

Are we straying into the dangerous territory of selling policies to the highest bidder? The policy-making process plays a pivotal role in the quality and substance of a democracy, but increasingly policies in South Africa seem to be hammered together informally, outside democratic institutions and away from public scrutiny. Also, since 1999, new centres of influence on policy-making – outside the elected representative system – have been established. Key among these are the presidential working groups: big business, black business, trade unions, agriculture, the international investment advisory council and international IT council. Significant policies had their genesis or were fleshed out in these presidential groups and were presented to parliament and the public as a fait accompli.

For the ANC leadership to restore public confidence – and convince people that we are not going down the dead-end road where money buys policy and access to senior leaders – nothing less than releasing the names of all the members of the 'progressive business forum' and declaring the amounts they have donated is needed. In fact, the ANC should go further. It should release the names of all individuals, businesses and foreign governments that donated money to the ANC over this electoral term.

Furthermore, new laws should be devised to regulate party funding. It is crucial to the health of our democracy that a donation to the ruling party does not buy favours. Unfortunately, the ANC's 'progressive business forum' is just another symptom of the dangerous slide of our democracy into one where those with the most money, the 'platinum class', determine public priorities. No wonder those without means increasingly look towards populist leaders in the hope that they will finally get their voices heard.

SA Reconciliation Barometer, Vol. 5, Issue 1, May 2007

When two value systems clash

At the heart of South Africa's moral decay, rampant corruption and public service delivery failures is the fact that the country is governed by two governance systems which are often contradictory. On the one hand there is the official governance system – the

South African Constitution, underpinned by a clear democratic framework – on the other hand there is the ANC's unofficial governance system – which is supposedly also underpinned by a democratic framework (although driven by liberation ideology).

The reality is that the ANC's governance system is essentially disintegrating, and because the ANC is the dominant political party this breakdown has spilled over into broader society. However, this (broken) ANC framework is seen by many cadres as far more important than the Constitution or pronouncements by the judiciary or any watchdog institution. This often means that, if judged by South Africa's constitutional framework, an ANC leader might be deemed to be corrupt. But unless he is also judged to be so by the leadership aristocracy that implements the ANC's corroded 'unofficial' liberation ideology framework, there will be no consequences.

Ironically, the ANC leadership elite expect ordinary citizens to adhere to the official governance system – the country's democratic Constitution – while they see themselves as bound only by the party's (broken) governance system. According to this system flawed political leaders like Jacob Zuma are essentially fine, even if their personal moral behaviour is appalling and their public views and actions go against constitutional values.

The challenge for genuinely democratically minded ANC members is how to replace this corrupted system with that set out in South Africa's Constitution. Sadly, within the ANC leadership aristocracy there appears to be little awareness of this corrosion. Furthermore, some genuinely democratically minded members and supporters of the ANC seem to think the problem lies with a few rotten apples. They argue incorrectly that if a certain leader, or leaders, is replaced, the 'democratic roots' of the ANC's liberation ideology system will magically sprout again.

Other genuinely democratically minded ANC members have given up. They say it is too late – the ANC's corroded governance system is now too embedded in the party's DNA. For them it would be better to break up the ANC and start afresh. Those who think it can still be changed must now stand up and defend South Africa's Constitution each and every time it is breached by the ANC's leadership aristocracy – to show that it trumps the current ANC system. And those outside the ANC must also do the same – and so build a critical mass in defence of South Africa's official constitutionally based governance system.

Rapport, 20 October 2011

An infant democracy

A loud and angry nation

South Africans appear to be turning into a nation of rude, intolerant people. It seems we have lost our ability to debate civilly, without angrily trying to humiliate each other into silence.

Recently the national chairman of the Umkhonto weSizwe Military Veterans' Organisation, Kebby Maphatsoe, issued a statement in which he said that former education minister Kader Asmal must go to the 'nearest cemetery and die'. Alarmingly, incidents like this appear to have become a 'normal' way of responding to a difference of opinion – Maphatsoe was responding to Asmal's rather mild criticism of the present African National Congress (ANC) government.

Responding to views that differ from one's own in a civil way is, of course, simply good manners. The tone in which leaders and individual citizens respond to being confronted with viewpoints that differ from their own is often a good indicator of the health of a democracy. In South Africa today decency, politeness and respect for the views of others appear to be on the wane. Many think that the only way to get their point across is to shout, to insult and to humiliate others. It is not only national leaders that are at fault; all kinds of disagreements – be they between individuals, family members or sections of a community – are now dealt with by shouting insults, in an attempt to humiliate those with which one disagrees. So ingrained has the culture of shouting to be heard become that some government leaders appear to only attend to the needs of constituencies when they shout at them, through (violent) protests.

In a democracy we have to be able to disagree respectfully, whether we are arguing with family members, others in our communities or politicians. No good can come from shouting: no proper policy can be worked out, priorities cannot be inclusively decided on, no consensus can be cobbled together.

Leadership also appears to be seen, wrongly, as made up of those who can shout the loudest and appear to be the most bellicose. It seems that many think that politicians who attempt to annihilate those that disagree with them – by assassinating their character, or calling their reputation and credibility into question – have 'strong' leadership qualities.

As South Africans we appear not to have mastered the art of disagreeing decently. Having disagreements over different opinions and viewpoints – both within one's own family as well as in political parties and across the broader nation – is perfectly natural and normal. What is important is how these differences are expressed and managed. Violently – whether verbally or physically – attacking those who disagree with you is neither good manners, nor is it in the spirit of democracy.

Democratic societies need to talk about their problems, in order to solve them. It is impossible to have informed debates or discussions in an atmosphere of rage. If we are not civil to each other in our interactions – whether these are on an individual, community or political level – solving society's myriad problems will be an impossible task. Our democracy will remain of low quality unless we determinedly push civility, respect and decency back to the centre stage of our everyday and public life.

Sowetan, 19 November 2009

Why dissent is crucial

Many government leaders have been caught off guard by the seemingly random and spontaneous protests by local communities frustrated by the snail's pace of service delivery and often indifferent local representatives. The immediate response has been to use the iron fist and send a few intelligence agents to weed out the local 'hotheads' and critics. Certainly, there is almost never a case to support violence to press demands in a democracy, but it is also true that the response of any government to the suffering of people often depends on the pressure that is put on it.

The great Indian economist Amartya Sen has shown how criticism, open public debate and dissent play a crucial role in preventing economic disasters such as famine or social unrest. Neglected issues, in this case slow delivery and callous public representatives, must be raised openly in public – without the threat of official retribution or censure, either from the ANC or the state.

Sen, for example, shows how in India the two neglected issues, gender equity and elementary education, only got the necessary official attention after repeated public protests and criticism of the government's record by its own supporters, social movements and the opposition. So, freedom of expression and discussion are not only crucial in pinpointing economic and social needs, but are also important in deciding on what needs should have priority.

It seems that the importance of open dialogue is often underestimated in South Africa, yet it is crucial in working out the kind of values we want to live by in our new democracy. For example, is it more important to give the poor a basic income grant or to focus on building entrepreneurs in the informal business sector? Or should we build a large black 'big business' class, hoping that their newfound wealth trickles down to the masses? These choices cannot be made by those in power – the people must decide. But this does not happen. The official line is that government must govern, and cannot waste time debating policy choices. The implication is that consulting with the masses will only bog down policies and delay their implementation.

A case in point: government decides centrally to build homes, but without asking the beneficiaries what kind of homes they want (obviously within the budget constraints) and where they should be. The recipients of the new homes, instead of being happy with them, complain about shoddy workmanship, distance to workplaces and lack of amenities. Few public officials listen, and if they do, they often respond with incredulity: did not government satisfy the citizens' housing needs by providing them with homes? All too frequently the bottled-up frustration of those ignored reaches a level where it spills over into violence.

Another obvious consequence of stifling public questioning of policies and government action is the flight of skills. President Mbeki often complains that there aren't enough senior people with the right skills to do specific jobs in government. Thus, we frequently see the same people being shifted from one post to the other at senior government levels. Lack of capacity, meaning not enough competent people at the top, is blamed when things go wrong in government, but many competent, skilled people, including ANC members, have been quickly marginalised for being critical of policies or arguing for alternatives. In the end, they have either no appetite for government office, or are just never again considered for crucial positions.

Sunday Independent, 20 March 2005

ANC no longer servants of the people

The constitutional requirement that ordinary citizens should be involved in decision making is now in danger of becoming a principle on paper only. The astonishingly glib way in which the ANC leadership dismissed calls from the public to debate the decision whether to close down the Scorpions, the country's most effective crime-busting unit, is a case in point.

The National Assembly's Portfolio Committee for Safety and Security is preparing to process two draft bills, the South African Police Service Amendment Bill and the National Prosecuting Authority Bill that aims to close down the Scorpions and incorporate its members into a new organised crime unit within the police service. The public have been invited to give their views on the closure of the Scorpions in public hearings to debate these bills.

117

Yet Yunus Carrim, the chairman of the portfolio committee on justice, has insisted that the decision to close down the Scorpions has already been taken and that the decision will not be reversed, regardless of what ordinary citizens say in the public hearings. Carrim was quoted as follows in *The Star*: 'Why can't you understand that even if the entire country were to say no, it is possible that a party could choose to say yes.'

This one sentence lays bare just how extraordinarily indifferent and arrogant many in the ANC leadership have become. They are no longer servants of the people. Carrim then said that the decision to disband the Scorpions was taken by more than 4 000 ANC delegates who represent 'about 750 000 ANC members'.

In a moment of extraordinary lucidity, no doubt induced by his sacking as premier of the Western Cape, Ebrahim Rasool laid his finger on the problem. He said in an interview with the *Sunday Times* that the ANC leadership fails to understand that the ANC is 'the driver of the nation', not 'the nation itself'. If the ANC fulfils the role of 'driver of the nation', one would expect it to get mandates for policies from the nation.

But right now, the core leadership of the ANC mistakenly thinks that whatever they do or say is what the nation would be doing or saying. If the ANC leadership, or a faction within it, decides to close down the Scorpions, then this is what the nation 'wants', since the ANC in its own mind believes it is the nation. The ANC thinks that because it was elected to govern in 2004, it can essentially do whatever it wants, without having to listen to the views of those who elected the party, at least until the next elections.

The reality is that the leadership of the ANC has become an exclusive club that prioritises its own personal and factional interests, disguising it as in the interest of the nation. They do not care about consulting or debating with anyone outside their club. What binds the members of this ANC leadership club together is the goal to make the hopelessly compromised ANC President Jacob Zuma the country's next president, even if it means razing the country to ashes.

The many successes of the Scorpions in fighting high-level corruption and crime was a glimmer of hope in a country faced with a crime wave that undermines the rule of law and public confidence in the police. The truth is that the ANC's closure of the Scorpions is but a smokescreen. Whatever mistakes the Scorpions made, it does not warrant closing down the unit. Instead, democratic oversight over this unit and all other security, intelligence and military agencies can rather be increased.

In 2006 the Constitutional Court made a series of seminal judgements on the duty of government to listen to ordinary citizens. Constitutional Court Judge Sandile Ngcobo, in his Doctors for Life judgement, insisted that it was a constitutional requirement that there had to be public debate about the merits of legislation before it could be passed in parliament. Ngcobo said that when the constitutional assembly drafted the Constitution, it never intended to limit ordinary citizens' participation in political decision making to their right to vote.

Ngcobo said not involving ordinary citizens in the law-making process would render laws invalid. The ANC leadership should heed this message.

The Witness, 31 July 2008

Transform but keep the judiciary independent

It is not easy to be a judge or magistrate in South Africa today. South Africa's judiciary faces mounting pressure to become more representative of the country's diverse population, adopt a new system of values based on the post-apartheid democratic Constitution, enforce the rights set out in that Constitution and keep the country's executive in check. Not surprisingly, not everyone believes they are up to the task.

However, recent public attacks on the judiciary by political factions have raised fears that its independence and integrity could be damaged, and confidence in the institution eroded. For example, last year supporters of the sacked former deputy president Jacob Zuma – who is fighting allegations of inappropriate behaviour – lashed out at the Supreme Court of Appeal for a relatively minor error in the summarised version of a subsidiary judgement. When, a year before, a judge sentenced Zuma's close confidant Schabir Shaik to jail for fraud and corruption, and criticised the 'symbiotic relationship' between the two men, some of Zuma's supporters labelled the (white) judge a 'racist'. A few years ago a black judge, John Hlophe, complained publicly that some of his white colleagues were racists.

The ruling ANC has recently released a package of proposals to transform the judiciary, including that the executive set court rules and control their budgets. It is obvious that not only do these proposals go against the important principle of the separation of powers, but also, if implemented, will undermine the independence of the judiciary. Although the ANC made it quite clear that it was not about to usurp the constitutionally entrenched principle that the judiciary should be independent, the proposals do cause legitimate concern.

The proper functioning of South Africa's constitutional democracy depends on an independent judiciary. Under apartheid, the majority of the country's population did not see the judiciary as either fair or independent. Barring a few credible exceptions, judges and magistrates enforced the apartheid system. During South Africa's Truth and Reconciliation Commission investigation into the human rights abuses committed during apartheid, the judiciary refused to come clean. This reinforced perceptions that the system was compromised. An integral part of the constitutional negotiations that brought the end of apartheid was an all-party agreement that, in spite of the judiciary's failings during the apartheid era, there would be no purge, and that its independence was crucial to establishing the rule of law in the new democratic atmosphere.

Changes were expected to be introduced in a way that retained the legitimacy of the judiciary. After all, South Africa's judiciary – especially the Constitutional Court – is now at the forefront of setting ethical values, moral standards and acceptable norms of behaviour in our infant democracy. For example, the relationship between politics and business is not only often blurred, but there has also been a revolving door between the two occupations. A court decision was needed to warn businessmen and -women that using their political connections to secure government contracts is wrong and can lead to lengthy imprisonment. Before that, party leaders showed no conviction in dealing with this corrosive issue.

In another case, the government for years refused to distribute life-giving antiretroviral drugs. The courts had to compel the government to meet its obligations to the sick and the poor. Even on the issue of basic social services, such as building homes for the needy, the courts have often forced the government to deliver.

There is no silver bullet for transforming South Africa's judiciary.

Obviously there should be credible public participation, and reform may need to come from within, but however it is done it must be in a way that does not threaten its integrity, independence and legitimacy.

The Washington Post, 28 March 2007

Change outdated attitudes to avoid 'second' rape

Obsolete public attitudes are as much a hurdle as shortcomings in the justice system in dealing effectively with the distressingly high incidence of rape. A fundamental part of transforming our society into an equal, caring and just one involves changing public attitudes.

The good thing about the Jacob Zuma rape trial is that it brings widely held attitudes – usually only spoken about in private, but which lie at the heart of much of the violence against women – out into the open. For one, it has laid bare the widely held, but patently wrong-headed belief that as a man you are entitled to own or possess a woman – a belief sometimes fig-leafed opportunistically behind tradition or culture.

As a democracy, we are trying to shift from a male-dominated patriarchal society to a new social order based on equality between men and women. Our challenge is to redefine masculinity – which is often wrongly viewed in macho terms, as underlined by phrases such as 'the man is the head of the house' – in this new democratic context.

On the evidence, we are clearly failing quite badly. It appears that many people, including members of the police service, judges and lawyers, believe that women are in part or completely responsible for being raped. For example, such downright archaic attitudes as 'she wore a short skirt' or 'she did not cross her legs properly' and was therefore 'asking for it' appear to be widely held. Clearly, if we are going to deal with the high incidence of rape in our country, we must change such attitudes.

A case in point is the law that deals with rape, the Sexual Offences Act, which was enacted in 1957, when the country's rulers were not only all white but also all male. The law uses a narrow definition of rape, and court procedure often puts the onus on the already traumatised victim to prove that she did not provoke her assailant.

New draft legislation, which would provide a more protective legal environment for rape victims, has been passed back and forth, like a yo-yo, between government departments and parliamentary committees since 1998. This not only shows how callous and indifferent our democratic institutions often are, but is also a reflection of official attitudes to rape. Clearly, a sense of urgency is lacking.

The question then is: what can we do to help rape victims cope with their second 'rape' – their harrowing ordeal in the criminal justice system? A very obvious start would be to foster a more sensitive attitude in the police service and put restrictions on victims being cross-examined about their sexual history in courts. It would also help if the police increased the number of special rape investigative units, took rape awareness training seriously and made easily available safe places where victims can be interviewed, counselled and medically examined.

Furthermore, judges should limit intrusive and overaggressive questions by defence teams. The importance of expert witnesses in every rape trial – to dispel myths about victims' behaviour, such as 'she did not report the incident immediately to the police', therefore 'she must have consented' – is absolutely crucial. However obvious this may seem, it does appear that many in the criminal justice system often fail to grasp why a victim might not report a rape for many weeks or months. For many, such behaviour is puzzling – as we saw during the Zuma trial – and it is often used by the defence as a basis for questioning, in order to make victims appear unreliable and untruthful.

Ultimately, we must create a space that allows every rape to be properly reported. To do this, we must battle outdated attitudes as these make reporting the crime more traumatic – with the victim having to battle a hostile criminal justice system. Without this, most victims will continue to suffer in silence.

Sunday Independent, 16 April 2006

The role of churches in challenging times

As moral decay, rampant corruption and public service delivery failures become more prevalent every day, the church – one of the few organised forces in civil society that can offer alternative leadership – has sadly been either co-opted by corrupt political leaders or has remained silent on the sidelines.

Instead of giving direction in these uncertain times, many churches, particularly those who had openly aligned themselves to the struggle against apartheid, are finding it hard to create a new role for them.

In March a group of mainstream church leaders, organised under Kairos Southern Africa, presented a document – 'Theological and Ethical Reflections on the 2012 Centenary Celebrations of the African National Congress (ANC): A word to the ANC in these times' – to the ANC's National Executive Committee. In it they criticised widespread corruption, the hostility to even the most polite criticisms and the astonishing lack of accountability by some ANC leaders. This was a step in the right direction.

Alarmingly, church pulpits are increasingly being used to fight ANC factional battles. On Easter Sunday, suspended ANC Youth League president Julius Malema was given a platform at the Last Move Ministries in Butterworth, asking the church to pray for him because 'those that used to be our friends have turned against us. They have not only turned against us but plan our death'. Malema said, to applause from congregants, 'You have an obligation, bishop, that what they plan for does not succeed.'

Die Burger newspaper reported that a pastor, speaking at a Workers' Day rally held in Athlone, Cape Town, last year, said 'Jesus was 'n kommunis' (Jesus was a communist), 'God het President Jacob Zuma as staatshoof gesalf' (God anointed President Jacob Zuma) and that the ANC, COSATU and the SACP were the 'Heilige Drie-eenheid' (Holy Trinity).

Also last year, Zuma said at a voter registration drive in Mthatha: 'When you vote for the ANC, you are also choosing to go to heaven. When you don't vote for the ANC you should know that you are choosing that man who carries a fork . . . who cooks people.' Zuma added, 'When you are carrying an ANC membership card, you are blessed. When you get up there, there are different cards used but when you have an ANC card, you will be let through to go to heaven.'

Jo Seoka, the president of the SA Council of Churches (SACC), responded rightly by saying, 'We work on a daily basis with scores of people who are hungry, unemployed and homeless. Offering heaven to these people while their suffering continues here on earth is escapist. We [the church and government] are expected to transform the livelihoods of all for the better.'

The reality is that in South Africa, as in many other African countries, one's credibility as an individual or an institution depends heavily on which side you were on during the liberation struggle, at least in the eyes of the former oppressed majority. The predominantly white churches who were seen as supporting apartheid and the black churches who remained silent, saying the church should not be involved in 'politics', have found themselves in a predicament in the new South Africa. Whenever they condemn the excesses of the ANC government, they are quickly reminded of their complicity with the previous regime.

However, what appears to be happening in the new dispensation is that these churches either remain silent out of guilt, or they become overly loyal and uncritical of the actions, even wrong ones, of the new political leaders, to curry favour. Sadly, in South Africa, the churches with 'struggle' credentials, those who supported the anti-apartheid struggle, have also mostly fallen silent as former comrades, now in government, backslide in the new South Africa. Many, such as Frank Chikane, lost his voice after joining the government and mainstream politics.

Worse still, the ANC government appears to be actively 'icing out' former comrades in the churches who are outspoken in the same way they were critical of the apartheid government. Even former president Thabo Mbeki had silenced churches and leaders who were in the anti-apartheid movement by co-opting them into his religious working group, where he expected them to raise their concerns 'privately', rather than publicly criticise the ANC government.

The Zuma presidency also appears to have totally silenced former anti-apartheid churches by securing the support of churches which were generally not part of the ANC's anti-apartheid alliance prior to 1994.

Many African liberation and independence movements, once in power, see civil society, including churches, as appendages of the party. Many of these movements demand uncritical loyalty from civil groups, particularly when church groups, trade unions and the press were their allies in the struggle for independence. In such instances, these African liberation movements impose a quasi 'state theology', co-opting many churches to serve the government's agenda. These churches are expected to be loyal to government and to become *imbongis* (praise singers) and give it credibility, even if the government is morally bankrupt. In return, church leaders receive patronage from government.

The influence of Christianity and the church on the ANC during the struggle is often forgotten. Many of the ANC's leaders, including its first president John Dube, its post-Second World War president Albert Luthuli and its president in exile, Oliver Tambo, were deeply influenced by the democratic message of the gospel: genuine democracy, morality and ethics. A major achievement of the ANC was that it managed to turn the struggle against apartheid into a moral struggle. This was one of the reasons why Western churches strongly backed the ANC from the 1980s onwards and generously provided funds and solidarity, also lobbying their governments to put pressure on the apartheid government.

The ANC has had an extraordinary number of capable church-men and lay clergymen who cut their organisational teeth within the church. These include Dube, Luthuli and Tambo, as well as leaders such as Allan Boesak, Desmond Tutu and Frank Chikane. The Christian strand within the ANC included liberation theologians (Chikane, Boesak and Tutu), Christian socialists (Tambo) and Christian democrats (Luthuli and James Calata).

But, clearly, democrats and ethical values in general are under threat in the ANC today. This can be seen in the public attacks on Tutu by the ANC leadership when he questions the direction the ANC takes on certain issues.

Apartheid has left both black and white South Africans with a feeling of 'existential insecurity'. Many black South Africans' sense of self was destroyed by the humiliations of apartheid. Many white South Africans' sense of self was equally battered by the fact that the 'familiar and trusted' institutions of their life under apartheid are now seen as part of a crime against humanity. Apartheid has not only left a broken society, it has also left broken individuals.

Many black and white South Africans experience a void but, sadly, the churches have been mostly unsuccessful in filling this emptiness. In some cases it has been filled by an obsessive materialism or cultural fundamentalism. Democrats would want to fill the void with the best elements of cultural, religious and spiritual values. However, as Pierre du Toit and Hennie Kotze have argued in their fascinating book entitled *Liberal Democracy and Peace in South Africa*, this 'existential insecurity' has generated illiberal attitudes in our society in the form of violent crime, a low level of tolerance for difference, xenophobia, social conservatism, and so on.

Kairos Southern Africa, in their document presented to the ANC, argues that the church cannot remain neutral and focus only on 'the preaching of the gospel', based on the argument that faith and spiritual life can somehow be 'separated' from the rest of our daily life. Churches should hold government and political leaders accountable and should at all times speak out against social injustice. Furthermore, individual church leaders should be more exemplary in their personal behaviour and set an example of an ethical and value-based leadership style as an alternative to the conduct of many politicians.

Our church will also have to internalise democratic values and rid themselves of racism, sexism and patriarchy within their own structures. To regain their credibility among black South Africans churches that supported apartheid in any way, they should publicly apologise for their actions in the past – and play an active role in holding the current and future governments account.

South Africa is at a tipping point. We face an uncertain future if churches and civil society groups do not intervene now. At some point, it may become too late to reverse the decline.

Sowetan, 28 May 2012

The ABC of being the SABC

Such is the crisis of confidence in the South African Broadcasting Corporation (SABC) now that perhaps the only way to restore public trust in the 'public broadcaster' is to set up an independent commission to investigate the public service obligations of the SABC in a constitutional democracy.

When faced with a similar crisis in the post-war period, the Pilkington Committee, looking into the transformation of the British Broadcasting Corporation (BBC), argued: 'The concept of broadcasting has always been of a service, comprehensive in character, with the duty of a public corporation of bringing to public awareness the whole range of . . . activity and expression developed in society.'

A commission of inquiry staffed by competent and impartial experts could offer a blueprint for an SABC which appears uncertain not only over how to exercise its public broadcasting role, but also what its relationship with government and the ruling party should be. In 1936, faced with technological changes that had transformed the face of broadcasting, the Ullswater Committee of inquiry proposed that due to 'the influence of broadcasting upon the mind and speech of the [British] nation', there was an 'urgent necessity . . . that the broadcasting service should at all times be conducted in the best possible manner and [to] the best possible advantage of the people'.

This has often been the route to redemption for ailing public broadcasters in other countries. For example, since 1923 the BBC has had several important independent commissions of inquiry to re-assess the role of that public broadcaster when political, economic and technological changes threatened the organisation.

The relationship between the public broadcaster and the state is always going to be complex, especially in a developing country, because broadcasting has such a far-reaching effect on the life of a nation. Striking a balance in reporting and programming that would keep the myriad interests of our diverse nation happy is an enormous challenge, but the emphasis should be firmly on presenting a range of views rather than that of the party in government – or even the dominant view of one faction within the party, or that of the president or any other leading group in society. In our case, for example, public interest in the Aids debate should be very clear. Thousands are dying and the cumulative effect on the country's economy, social fabric and health care services is devastating. It is in the public interest for journalists to ask critical questions and for broadcasters to produce quality programmes showing the reality of this disease.

The public service role of the SABC is currently mostly measured by whether it produces quality programming and practises good journalism, and by the level of its independence from government, business or other dominant interests. The SABC's record is not very inspiring in this regard, but in a developing country enlightening the public is surely even more crucial. In a country where large numbers of people haven't had access to a decent education, broadening minds with programmes of quality, which reflect cultural diversity and educate audiences politically and socially, is imperative. This is an area where the SABC has failed dismally. South Africa does not have the luxury of building a new nation on the grounds of shared culture, ethnicity or language. Our national identity will have to be built in the political sphere and underpinned by institutions that everyone identifies with and feels they have a stake in. The SABC is one of these national institutions.

For this identity building to happen, national institutions need to be trusted by the majority of South Africans. If their integrity is in question, the public lose trust in them and their ability to be tools for positive change is diminished. Sadly, the SABC is afflicted with the same malaise as all the other national institutions. The SABC board should protect the institution against political interference, ensure that it provides quality journalism and programming and be held accountable for any mismanagement, but the reality is that the old board was completely discredited and the new one is already dead in the water.

The board selection process is vulnerable to political influence. One way to transform it is by setting up an independent commission to select the majority of the board members. A quarter of the nominees could, for example, go through a political process – in which parliament, government and opposition parties can participate – but the rest must be appointed independently.

SABC bosses regularly argue that the organisation receives unfair criticism from the print media. They may be right, but this kind of criticism is one of the ways in which the SABC is held to account, which is especially important when its board has a history of failing as an oversight mechanism.

State funding to the SABC is limited, yet the organisation is expected to produce quality programming and adapt to new technology. Unless it gets more public money, the SABC will be forced to look increasingly towards maximising advertising revenue, and chasing profits in this kind of environment can lead to cutbacks in staff and programming quality. Instead, more government investment is needed alongside a renewed commitment to editorial professionalism.

There is always going to be a conflict between the government, the media and civil society over what is in the public interest. Right now the SABC is just too close to the state – which in itself stifles innovation and encourages conformity. Acting in the public interest means that the SABC cannot choose sides in political battles. To act in the public interest, is 'to be free from all sectional interests, including that of government'. In the end the values of the Constitution, and the fact that our country is a participatory and representative democracy, should guide the SABC's approach whenever it is uncertain – as it appears it is now.

The Witness, 22 September 2007

Why ANC supporters always go back for more

Before elections ANC supporters embark on massive public protests, complaining about poor public service delivery, corruption and indifference by elected ANC representatives and government officials. Yet, in elections they vote for the same ANC. Soon thereafter they are back on the streets, venting their anger once again at the very ANC representatives for which they voted. Why?

Many ANC supporters vote for the ANC as a movement, rather than for individual ANC candidates. This is why a compromised leader like Jacob Zuma can be elected as ANC president. ANC voters who were opposed to Zuma were unable to separate him from the ANC as a party.

The ANC has been successful in blaming poor performance on individual rotten apples, rather than the movement as a whole, and many ANC supporters reckon corrupt and incompetent leaders in the ANC are a small minority. They argue their movement is still overwhelmingly led by those who are capable and committed, and the prominence of sensible individual ANC leaders, such as Deputy President Kgalema Motlanthe, reassures the doubtful.

As a banned organisation the ANC operated like a broad church – something it still does to this day – providing emotional sustenance to members and direction to their lives. Often church members may have problems with parts of a service or their local pastor, but it is difficult for them to cut their ties with the church – and so it is for many ANC members.

The ANC has transferred its organisational model of patronage, from its time as a liberation movement, directly to its current position as the ruling party in government and many poor ANC supporters think only the ANC can provide them with 'patronage' – jobs, public services and welfare. They perceive predominantly white parties as either hostile to or uninterested in the issues of blacks – jobs, decent and accessible housing and education – and other black parties as insignificant. Many ANC supporters genuinely fear that leaving the ANC will mean even further marginalisation.

The alliance partners of the ANC – the Congress of South African Trade Unions (COSATU), the South African Communist Party (SACP), civic and civil society organisations – help keep voters on their side. Regular criticism of government by COSATU leaders, for instance, provides an outlet for disillusioned ANC members – reassuring them that others share their worries – and allows them to remain within the ANC fold.

Critically, many believe that the ANC's poor governance can be resolved by electing a new leader or leaders, or by adopting 'pro-poor' policies. Yet, such is the rot within the ANC now that only root-and-branch reform can change it for the better. It will not happen simply by replacing individual leaders and certain policies.

Inequality runs along racial lines in South Africa and opportunistic ANC leaders have been very effective in reminding desperate supporters that it is because of the legacy of apartheid rule that they remain stuck in poverty. And how, when confronted with this 'truth', could an ANC supporter be convinced to cast his vote for another party?

Opposition parties must be seen to care about the issues important to the black poor: jobs, affordable housing and education. In places where these parties govern, they must show publicly that they are governing not only well, but also in the interests of blacks – this will break existing perceptions that only the ANC governs in the interests of blacks.

The opposition must also, collectively, make the case more convincingly that it is not only individual ANC members that are corrupt, but that the rot runs much deeper. And a grand coalition, combining all of South Africa's opposition parties, may also help to create the perception that there is a possible alternative to the ANC, an alternative which can offer its own forms of patronage.

Rapport, 10 January 2012

The flaws in our party political system

Five years on and it appears that little has changed. Those curious creatures called politicians, with their shiny shoes, fancy suits and plastic smiles, were again traipsing along the potholed, unpaved and often garbage-strewn township streets to exhort wary residents to exercise their democratic right to vote.

Not surprisingly, many were rather quick to trumpet the 49% voter turnout, as a soothing improvement on the 48% notched up in the local poll back in 2000. True, but this number is still a long way short of the 90% plus voter turnout in the 1994 election. And even leaving this uncomfortable truth aside, all the clever number crunching cannot hide the fact that a lot more people who voted this time around spoilt their ballots – to show how cross they are with the political system.

If there's one thing that local elections show time and again, it is that political parties are failing the South African people. To start with, choice is in short supply, in spite of the array of parties listed on the ballot – most of the parties are just too similar. Quality is an even scarcer commodity. Promises are made which are hardly kept. Politicians are unaccountable. Some are just downright corrupt. Others appear to be under the delusion that they are more important than the people that elected them. Indeed, they seem to believe they are the masters of the voters, rather than their servants. Taking this into account, it can come as no surprise that turnouts are dropping, that the young are apathetic, elected representatives and public institutions distrusted and party membership declining – in the heady months after its unbanning in 1990 the ANC had a membership of around one million, now it is less than 150 000, and dropping fast.

It is not that ordinary people have switched off politically; it is the political parties that are alienating them. Ordinary people do care about their communities – about the bread-and-butter issues, such as poor schools, unsafe and unreliable public transport, crime and grime and dysfunctional neighbourhoods – and large numbers of people are still involved in community groups of one form or another. Clearly, the problem lies with formal politics.

The lack of relevant opposition parties in South Africa is a problem, since the quality of any democracy is hugely dependent on a robust opposition. Our opposition parties are not meek – they loudly and regularly criticise the government – but whether they are relevant is another matter. To be relevant, parties must reflect the political views of a large tranche of the population. So, in South Africa, opposition parties must represent the black voter if they are to strengthen our democracy.

Unfortunately, even now, the opposition parties are unattractive, irrelevant and disconnected to the majority. And, what is worse, beyond the cosmetic they are not even seriously contemplating reinventing themselves. In fact, listening to the leaders of all parties – including those of the ruling ANC – it is hard to see that there will be significant changes going forward. It appears that it is going to be business as usual. This would be a mistake. The lesson from the local elections must be that it cannot be business as usual.

How are we going to restore trust in political parties? What kind of checks and balances should be instituted to prevent the fast-eroding public trust in politicians and political parties turning into a public disengagement with the democracy in general? There is a straightforward solution, but we will have to find a way to give citizens more direct power over political decisions and policies that affect them if we are to re-engage civil society. To start with, the closed party list system must be done away with. One cannot vote for an MP, mayor or councillor and not know his or her identity, politics or record beforehand.

Furthermore, the power of the executive and the presidency should be dramatically reduced, while that of parliament is boosted – thus giving it real teeth. Right now parliament is a rubber stamp – MPs are powerless against party bosses and committees are weak. People will regain confidence in politics and political parties only if they see their MPs and councillors are really serious about effecting change and have the power to do so.

Citizens must also have the right to initiate legislative processes, public inquiries and hearings into the behaviour of politicians, public bodies and their senior management. Furthermore, the public must be more involved in the creation of policies and laws and given a greater say over who is appointed to the boards of public bodies and companies, such as electricity utility Eskom. Moreover, these boards should include ordinary citizens and have consumer representation. In short, they must become accountable.

Those parties that get public funding should practise internal democracy. Since the taxpayer sponsors them, their internal governance must reflect the democratic norms of the Constitution. Democracy is not only about holding elections every five years, but also about ordinary people having a say in policy-making and having elected representatives that are accountable throughout the period between elections. If there is no change, violent protests are likely to be the norm – as ordinary people's bottled-up frustration spills over.

Moreover, more and more people will be tempted to seek refuge in divisive ethnic politics or be seduced by selfish politicians – blaming their marginalisation on their skin colour or ethnicity. The scenes outside Jacob Zuma's rape trial show how those who feel excluded from their party and the political system can be seduced by those who promise them an earthly paradise. This will continue to happen. Don't blame the people, blame their leaders and our political parties.

Cape Times, 20 March 2006

We need an opposition, but one with credibility

The Achilles heel of South Africa's democracy is the lack of a credible opposition party that speaks to the long-suffering black majority. In the absence of electoral competition, an extraordinary complacency has taken root in the ruling ANC. It is one of the main reasons for the country's deepening political crisis and it means that no matter how badly the ANC governs, the only way black voters can voice their dissatisfaction is by not voting in the next general election.

Despite the paucity of opposition parties, the attempt to reform the National Party is certainly not the answer. In 2004, what remained of the National Party merged with the ANC. Its last leader, Marthinus van Schalkwyk, is now minister of tourism in President Thabo Mbeki's cabinet. In spite of its record as the party that implemented apartheid, it would have been more beneficial for the National Party – which still managed to get almost a quarter of the vote in the 1994 elections – to continue its cautious move towards nonracialism and to remain an opposition party.

The Democratic Alliance (DA), the main opposition party, is outspoken and tackles government head-on about corruption, but beyond that has pitched itself mostly at white middle-class voters. The DA is silent on social justice issues and on high rates of unemployment and poverty, linked to apartheid engineering that left most blacks without skills, education or social capital to make headway in a modern industrial economy.

The main black opposition party, the Inkatha Freedom Party (IFP), was supported by Western leaders, including Margaret Thatcher and George Bush Snr, during the apartheid era. Back then the IFP was seen as a pliant pro-West bulwark against the pro-Soviet ANC. But today the IFP is on the verge of implosion, having failed to transform from a regional Zulu-nationalist and monarchist party into a national, nonracial party. On top of that, the ruling ANC is probably more Zulu than it is.

The Pan-Africanist Congress (PAC), the liberation movement that rivalled the ANC at the height of apartheid, has basically collapsed. This is mostly due to in-fighting and the pursuit of ZANU-PF-like extreme Africanist policies at a time when most black people just want a job, a home and decent education for their children.

Ironically, most of the real and effective opposition against government finds itself outside of parliament among new civil groups. It will make more sense for the opposition parties, whose policies do not differ much anyway, to merge into one block. Given the still open wounds of the struggle, any new party that wants to make inroads into the black vote must be led by leaders who played at least some role during the struggle.

Ultimately, the best solution for South Africa is a split in the tripartite alliance into a centre-left faction (currently rallied around President Thabo Mbeki) and a left faction (rallied around ANC President Jacob Zuma). It seems as though South African politics will only be infused with the electoral dynamism the country so desperately needs when the ruling party has to face a real possibility of losing an election.

The Independent, 29 August 2008

Talking frankly about race

Creating a new South African identity

The raging debate over what makes one South African, which currently focuses on whether a person is African enough, is simply wrong-headed. Sixteen years into our democracy the question we should be asking, is: Will we ever manage to create a shared national identity?

This country's bitter history of more than 350 years of colonialism and apartheid has engendered deep divisions along political, as well as cultural, linguistic and ethnic lines. Past repressive governments have insisted that South Africa is fundamentally a 'society of self-enforced communities, always potentially – and in the absence of the (colonial or apartheid) state, actually – in gruesome conflict with one another'.

As citizens, we ourselves sometimes cleave to the divisions of the past – making the forging of a shared new identity much harder, yet so much more urgent.

In a diverse country such as ours, our solution should not rest on a national identity based on a singular shared culture, language or ethnicity. Neither, as is often assumed in Western models of nationhood, should it rest on a common citizenship or shared geographic space alone. As Nelson Mandela stated from the dock in 1962, it also should not be defined solely in relation to one majority community.

South African identities are not 'gated communities' with fixed borders; more often than not, they overlap meaningfully, beyond the occasional shared word or value. Our modern South Africanness therefore cannot be but a 'layered', plural and inclusive one, and one based on acceptance of our 'interconnected differences'.

However, building commonality on the basis of difference presents a unique challenge. A shared sense of South Africanness will have to be based on politics. It will require continual persuasion and lobbying, and cannot be enacted by decree or be achieved through good intentions alone. This is both a weakness and a strength.

What, then, is the basis for our common political identity?

South Africa's unifying narrative is predominantly political: a history of emerging out of the ashes of a civil war and peacefully constructing a democratic dispensation. Therefore our Constitution, the founding document of our political settlement, anchors both our diversity and a new set of democratic rules and values. In addition, a common South Africanness should also be woven around the idea of an inclusive democracy. And solidarity with the most vulnerable must cut across racial and political divides – meaning that social justice should underpin governance.

Taken together, these would form the basis of our common interests and a national consensus across historical, ethnic, political and colour divides. Our shared ambition should be to mould a new democratic identity for South Africa that emphasises the present and future, rather than remaining trapped in the bitterness of the past.

Yet, because this common South Africanness is a political construct, there are some obvious pitfalls.

First, leadership style will matter very much. It will be an imperative for political leadership to govern in the interests of every South African at all times, and not for one political party or faction. Here, we can recall the legacies of Gandhi in India and Nelson Mandela, who in South Africa attempted to harness symbols of patriotism around which the whole nation could rally.

Further, with politics at the core of South Africanness, undermining democracy and the Constitution threatens the very foundations of this shared identity. Consequently, leaders must follow the rules applied to everyone else, and flagrant ignorance of new democratic laws on their part won't do. Democratic institutions (including the courts), the media and civil society must continue to be active watchdogs, ensuring that democratic and constitutional values are embedded in everyday practice.

Trust in, and the legitimacy of, the democratic system and its institutions are additional requirements for a strong common identity. Where corruption in the public sphere appears to go without punishment, or where consequences are mitigated by political connections to the ruling party, government's legitimacy and credibility are undermined.

It is also important that the vast talents of all South Africans are utilised, and that deliberate marginalisation or exclusion based on race is eschewed. Opportunistically using race for self-enrichment or to cover up wrongdoing undermines a common identity, as does retreating into 'nativism' and proffering exclusive definitions of South Africanness or Africanness.

Our common South African identity, and shared future, will have to be built as a mosaic of the best elements of our diverse present and past, histories and cultures. This does not mean committing identity or cultural suicide. We can still embrace our individual identities – as Afrikaners, Zulus, Indians – while also being part of the broader South African collective. However, there should not be only one way of practising Afrikaner-ness or Zulu-ness, and some amongst us may want the choice to opt out of these identities altogether, and this must be respected. Most importantly, the way we embrace and practise these identities in our daily lives must not conflict with the constitutional values of human dignity, gender equality and respect and empathy for others.

Race, and the continued legacy of apartheid's racial and economic inequalities, are responsible for major fault lines in the country's efforts to build a common South Africanness. Therefore, at the heart of economic development strategy must be policies that genuinely uplift not only the poor, but rather the widest number of people at the same time – rather than just a small elite, whether white or black.

Finally, if the poor black majority remains marginalised economically, a common South Africanness will remain a fading dream, as hardliners of all races continue to manipulate black resentment and white anxieties to push for a narrow definition of South Africanness which excludes others.

SA Reconciliation Barometer, Vol. 8, Issue 3, November 2010

No band-aid solution for South Africa's racial problems

Given South Africa's long and bitter history of racial oppression and its continued legacy, it is astonishing that the country is yet to have an open and transparent public discussion about race. In fact, the only people who talk publicly about race are the extremists, which seldom leads to rational debate. But without such a debate we will not be able to find lasting solutions to our problems and neither will we be able to agree on the basic elements of policies of redress.

Of course, we should not be imprisoned by the past, but we cannot simply argue to let bygones be bygones, as if 1994 was simply Year Zero, when we all started from the same slate in terms of education, property and social capital. The fact that economic inequalities still run along racial lines – with blacks mostly poor and whites mostly better off – is a real obstacle to genuine reconciliation, and South Africa's economic downturn will only increase tensions. Naturally, many whites who fall into economic difficulties will be tempted to blame a black-dominated African National Congress (ANC) government for being 'against' them. Poorer black South Africans may also be seduced into turning their anger on whites in general, rather than seeing it as a combination of the legacy of apartheid inequities and misguided policies by black-dominated democratic governments.

The impact that centuries of racism can have on a community, and individuals within that community, is often underestimated. Former president Thabo Mbeki, for instance, often responded in an exaggerated manner to perceived white prejudice. For example, he adopted his ineffective quiet diplomacy towards Zimbabwe partly because some white South Africans drew comparisons between

147

Zimbabwe's trajectory as a nation – under ZANU-PF – and what was happening in South Africa under the ANC. Ironically, Mbeki's quiet diplomacy – an overreaction to an outspoken group whose focus was, predominantly, the plight of white Zimbabweans – has helped to prolong Mugabe's autocratic rule and increase the suffering of the very people who had already felt the brunt of his tyranny – black Zimbabweans.

We should not hide behind racial solidarity to support often very undemocratic practices. For example, should the appointment of a black judge be applauded just because he or she is black, even if the judgements they hand down are blatantly against the letter of the Constitution? A case in point: it is well known that many black judges are as conservative as some of their old-style white colleagues when it comes to rape. These judges – black and white – still astonishingly blame the victims for being raped. Surely, in such cases, a black judge cannot be supported merely on the basis of his or her blackness?

To deal with racism we must also be able to point out when an unskilled or inexperienced black person is put in a position where they are not performing – rather than keep silent, because at least 'he or she is black'. Of course, competence is not a white preserve, either. Black excellence must be acknowledged. When blacks do well, it should not be dismissed as because of their 'political connections', and so on. White instances of incompetence cannot be ignored, either. The poor ultimately pay the price for incompetence, whether it is white or black incompetence.

The American scholar of race Cornel West warns against the pitfalls of what he calls a resort to black 'authenticity' politics, whereby every issue is reduced to 'racial reasoning'. He argues rightly that we must 'replace racial reasoning with moral reasoning, to understand the black-freedom struggle, not as an affair of skin pigmentation and racial phenotype but rather as a matter of ethical principles and wise politics'.

Shouting 'racism' to sideline rivals, for self-enrichment at the expense of the public good, or to deflect attention from our own wrongdoing is simply wrong – and will only increase racial tension.

To break down racial stereotypes, there has to be greater integration, whether in clubs, at social events or in community organisations. Joint action on all levels, whether in government or in school committees, can do much to break down racial misunderstanding. Children will have to be taught in schools about the negative effects of racial discrimination. But adults, especially in the workplace, must also be educated about it.

Whites will have to show a deeper understanding for the still very deep legacy of racial discrimination. Blacks will have to understand that whites have legitimate fears.

In the long term, lifting the living standards of the poorest will be one of the surest ways to boost black confidence – and reconciliation. In the short term, government must base the criteria for recipients of poverty-alleviation measures on the extent of their poverty, rather than on race. Because the majority of blacks are in absolute poverty, they would naturally be the majority of the recipients of these measures, but we must introduce a basic income grant for all families – black or white – that are desperately poor. Recipients of this grant could in turn be required to work in the community for a minimum period.

Affirmative action must be honestly implemented – in both the public and private sectors – and targeted to advance those who are genuinely poor. It should be suspended in sectors in the economy identified as high-growth areas, those areas critical to service

149

delivery and where there is a scarcity of skills. We should have a clear time frame for when the policy should be dropped.

Furthermore, we should abandon black economic empowerment (BEE) as a policy and reward predominantly white companies for investing in job creation, education, skills transfer and housing and for uplifting the physical and social infrastructure of townships and rural areas – as well as for supporting the five million-odd (mostly black) entrepreneurs in the informal sector. We must also demand that the beneficiaries of the current narrow BEE plough their capital back into economic development and eschew 'bling' culture and conspicuous consumption.

Finally, to tackle racism effectively demands honesty, courage, social justice and pragmatism. There should be no place for easy stereotyping, generalisations and prejudices – from either blacks or whites.

Sowetan, 6 May 2010

Give new meaning to transformation

As the country celebrates another year of our infant democracy, transformation has clearly become a buzz word. Yet it is hard to find much agreement on what is meant by this. On the available evidence, no matter which way we look at it, our record must at best be mixed. Perhaps we have arrived at a point where we need to question whether our vision of transformation remains relevant. Indeed, are we not still stuck in 1994?

For one, it does appear that transformation has now become a zero-sum numbers game. Yes, the most basic element of transformation is bringing blacks into positions – whether in the judiciary, the workplace or sporting teams – from which they were excluded during the apartheid era. But transformation is more than this. For example, is it transformation to allow a few black businessmen and -women – who really don't care about the redistribution of wealth to the black majority more broadly – to enrich themselves?

Currently only a very small group of people, often well connected to the upper echelons of the ANC, benefit from BEE. How does this address the problem of widening inequality?

Transformation should be about redistributing wealth more broadly. And if this is the case, would it not be better to introduce a basic income grant or an education grant to get children through school? Senior government figures, such as Finance Minister Trevor Manuel, have dismissed this as encouraging entitlement, but is making a few black tycoons fabulously rich for trading on their political connections or blackness any better?

Furthermore, transformation should be about the redistribution of not just capital but also skills and education. It should be about reducing the widening inequality gap on all levels, redistributing opportunities and securing equal chances for all.

Transformation should also be about changing values and attitudes. We need efficiency, accountability and responsibility. Democratic institutions should be accessible, friendly and efficient. Yet they are often indifferent, inaccessible and unresponsive. Public servants are invariably rude and inefficient, and elected representatives arrogant and unaccountable.

True transformation requires a move away from a society of blind obedience and mindless loyalty, qualities which stifle innovation

151

and entrepreneurship. Flexibility and adaptability are crucial if we are to renew our transformation vision.

Sunday Independent, 30 April 2006

It won't help to sprinkle black faces in high places

The unbridled joy at South Africa's Rugby World Cup triumph has been dampened by gloomier speculation that the winning squad is likely to be broken up and its coach sent packing, to make way for a new regime that will, through enforced government quotas, reflect all the colours of the rainbow nation.

Following colonialism and apartheid segregation, all South Africa's institutions must now become representative of the country's diverse population and adopt a new rights and value system based on the post-apartheid democratic Constitution. The word for this is 'transformation'. However, some black politicians are cynically using transformation – or the lack thereof – to score Brownie points. They want to grab the headlines by occasionally targeting a 'white' sport to compensate for poor performance. At the same time, some white politicians are using transformation as a bogey, to show that whites are under siege from a black government.

Transformation in itself is tricky enough, but South Africa's obsession with seeing it as only replacing white faces with black – be it in sporting teams, the judiciary, company boards or the workplace – is making real transformation even harder. The result of forcing the appearance of individual black faces at the top is less likely to lead to effective and lasting transformation.

Not surprisingly, black players are often caught in this no-man's-land: when teams lose, they are unfairly blamed; if the team wins, they hardly get any praise. The immediate consequence of this is that some black professionals are refusing to be seen as affirmative action candidates, whether in sport or in the workplace. Transformation, if it is to work, will have to have a bottom-up approach. It is imperative that access to finance, training, world-class facilities and support must be made available to black clubs, schools and universities.

However, grass-roots black rugby is totally under-resourced. Because of the emphasis on black faces, all the big clubs and provinces do is secure the best black players, and once they have them, they are not interested in grass-roots development. Those who are shouting the loudest for black quotas in the national rugby team do not appear to care about this terrible situation. But that is real transformation: it is harder, it takes longer, yet it will bring more sustainable results.

The same argument could be made for business transformation. The popular idea has been to create a few rich black businessmen quickly, such as Tokyo Sexwale, Cyril Ramaphosa and Saki Macozoma. However, for the five million black entrepreneurs who eked out a living during apartheid, government support, access to finance and training are all distant dreams.

Putting black faces in the national team or creating a few black business tycoons are band-aid measures. South African companies could have, for example, identified potential black talent in poor schools in 1994 and then supported them throughout their education. But very few 'adopt' a township club, school or community.

The government, too, has fallen far short. Sometimes its outbursts about the lack of transformation mask its own failure to build school and sporting infrastructure in poorer areas. For me, and many of my generation, afternoon sport and other activities gave new purpose to our lives. Now, school sports in many black communities have, in effect, stopped, because of the lack of resources and heavy teaching loads.

And the rot is not only in our schools. Take, for example, the national soccer team. It is managed in the main by black administrators, and has mostly black players drawn from predominantly black-owned clubs. However, because of the faulty view that soccer is now 'representative' of the make-up of the population, there is no government monitoring of the sport. The national under-23 team has not qualified for the Olympics, and the national team is in the doldrums. The former reservoir of the youth league, the Chappies League, has been closed. There are no organised youth structures. The management of the national soccer body is a national embarrassment. Yet, the government says nothing, even though South Africa will host the 2010 World Cup.

The issue should not be about perfectly representing all groups in a sporting team or company. It should be about the right of every individual, especially those from poor black areas, to be able to get the best support, training and finances to become world-beaters and to become part of teams or managements on the basis of their own abilities. This necessarily means that there are not always going to be perfectly representative teams of all races.

The challenge of transformation is to continue excellence, while making the country's sports, companies and institutions more representative. This will mean making transformation more broadly based. Getting it wrong, either by focusing only on supplanting white faces with black ones, or by doing nothing, will not only in-crease racial tensions and divisions, but will also put a brake on the development of the country.

The Independent, 24 October 2007

Facing the perceptions around affirmative action

Affirmative action remains one of the most explosive issues in South Africa today. If not handled with care, it could lead to racial po-larisation, not only between black and white but also within black communities.

Following colonial and apartheid-era racial discrimination, some form of redress for past injustices is needed. The affirmative action challenge is this: many whites are fearful that affirmative action will lead to reverse discrimination against them; many Africans fear that affirmative action is taking too long; while many Coloured and Indian communities fear they may be passed over again, this time because they are not 'dark' enough.

Ahead of the December conference, President Thabo Mbeki is now planning a new series of meetings with representatives from different communities who feel anxious about how affirmative ac-tion is implemented. Among those Mbeki is trying to find space for in his diary are Democratic Alliance (DA) leader Helen Zille, as well as with leaders from the Freedom Front Plus, Solidariteit and prominent leaders and organisations in Indian and Coloured communities.

South Africa's fragile attempts at reconciliation across the races are in danger, unless a middle way is found among these different perceptions. Mbeki, in his newsletter to ANC members last Friday, said the big problem was that 'we cannot get everyone to sing from the same hymn sheet on the important question of how to build a nonracial South Africa, and the role of affirmative action in this regard'. He rightly said there should be 'continuous examination and critical review' of affirmative action, because 'medium- and long-term stability of the country depended on visibly and meaningfully moving towards a nonracial society'.

The ANC's main discussion document dealing with this contentious issue, and which was prepared for the party's December 2007 national conference, concedes that the need for affirmative action 'will decline' as political and economical power becomes more evenly distributed between black and white South Africans.

Although Mbeki has often publicly emphasised the issues that divide the country more than those that could unite it, away from the public eye he has searched for a mutually acceptable compromise on affirmative action. Typically, he and his office have kept such efforts under wraps. In other instances, it has been overshadowed by his and other ANC leaders' sometimes ill-considered public statements on race relations, such as Labour Minister Membathisi Mdladlana's statement that affirmative action will go on until eternity.

Or Smuts Ngonyama, the head of the ANC presidency, who said that Coloureds (and Indians) suffered less under apartheid and thus should stand behind Africans in the affirmative action queue. The focus should not be on who suffered the most, but on how we reverse the appalling inequalities left by apartheid in all communities, targeting the most vulnerable but at the same time giving every South African the opportunity to flourish.

As part of his reforms to shift the ANC to the political centre and to promote reconciliation, the president has from mid-2000 wooed white Afrikaans-speaking groups such as Solidariteit and the Afrikaanse Handelsinstituut, as well as farming and language rights groups. A few months after his inauguration, Mbeki despatched the minister in the presidency, Essop Pahad, to look at ways to soothe the fears of white and black communities (Indians and Coloureds) who felt excluded. The idea was to put together a flexible affirmative action pact that would safeguard all communities.

When Mbeki persuaded New National Party (NNP) leader Marthinus van Schalkwyk to merge with the ANC in 2004, one of the main sweeteners was that the ANC agreed to an affirmative action pact that would protect whites from the negative aspects of affirmative action. However, in the light of the growing perception among black professionals that affirmative action has slowed in the private sector, some ANC leaders are now in favour of a stronger push of affirmative action by the ANC. Increasing community protests by ANC supporters who are angry about slow service delivery and economic redistribution have also exacerbated affirmative action tensions.

The ANC itself is deeply divided over the issue of affirmative action. ANC Western Cape Transport and Public Works MEC Marius Fransman's proposal for a moratorium on affirmative action – to attract scarce skills to the province – led to pandemonium in the ANC. Fransman had thought he was building on Mbeki earlier initiatives to search for an affirmative action 'CODESA'.

The first thing that should be done is to deal openly with black and white perceptions of affirmative action. There has to be more flexibility over how affirmative action is implemented. Fransman's proposal for a suspension of affirmative action in fields that require scarce skills is a good solution. The abuse of affirmative action policies

157

should also be stopped. Some government departments appoint people because of their political connections, rather than on merit. This drives not only whites away, but also blacks who believe they do not have the right political connections.

But it is not only the government that must provide leadership on affirmative action. Former DA leader Tony Leon often simplistically blamed South Africa's skills shortage on affirmative action. In her speeches, the DA's new leader Helen Zille has followed the same line. The challenge for the DA is to provide both a credible alternative to affirmative action and to show, as its CEO Ryan Coetzee puts it, 'that it cares just as much for black as for white issues'.

Yet the DA pushes the idea that affirmative action discriminates against whites, Coloureds and Indians. The Inkatha Freedom Party (IFP) has also called for a total rejection of affirmative action – this will probably chase away its last remaining black middle class supporters. Affirmative action is one of the issues that really show why both black and white opposition parties are not rising to the challenge to come up with innovative proposals on serious economic issues. Because of this, they will struggle to break the ANC juggernaut.

The Witness, 4 August 2007

Our everyday problems

Government should look crime in the face

Wherever you go in South Africa – from the still poorly policed townships and rural villages to the highly secure gated communities in the formerly white suburbs – crime is likely to crop up in conversation. Spiralling crime levels are battering citizens' confidence in government and to dismiss public outrage as sneeringly as Safety and Security Minister Charles Nqakula did, will not help matters.

Importantly, for many years government leaders, for a number of reasons, did not appear to rate crime as a priority. For a start, they live in well-guarded splendour, removed from the daily harassment ordinary citizens are subjected to. Secondly, government has been hiding behind the race issue, dismissing complaints about rising crime as whining by whites – though they do have a point in that if you read about crime in the media in some parts of the country you would think it only happens in white suburbs. The Democratic Alliance (DA) has focused on crime – which it should – but in a way that, at its most divisive, implies that whites are under siege from black criminals. But crime knows no race and not taking complaints over rising crime levels seriously – whether from blacks or whites – is a dereliction of government's responsibility to protect the lives of its citizens. This official arrogance, aloofness and lack of empathy are why people take to the streets to vent their anger and frustration.

Analyses often miss the link between deepening inequality and crime, but it should be obvious that crime rates are going to rise if you have a social mix where there is rising poverty in the midst of increasing opulence. The economy is growing at almost 6%, the white middle class is doing very well and the black middle class is booming, but those at the bottom have been left behind. The Aids pandemic has left many households without breadwinners, a situation compounded by the apartheid legacy of broken, displaced and traumatised communities. Government has refused to provide a basic income grant, because it says it will lead to a culture of entitlement – though fear that middle-class opinion will disapprove of them dispensing taxpayers' money to those out of work may be closer to the truth.

Surely, the social costs of not intervening, which include a rising crime rate, are more important than such worries. The way to deal with crime is to target criminals firmly but also to deal decisively with the social causes of crime, which means introducing a basic income grant to the indigent – something which is supported by most political parties, civil groups and churches. Simultaneously, the government should hire 100 000 or so new police assistants. Conscripts should be recruited from the unemployed in townships and working-class communities. They can be put on a crash course, not unlike the notorious *kitskonstabels* of the 1980s, although the new recruits will have a more noble role.

Furthermore, why does the police department not endorse a big recruitment drive in schools and universities, seek out those with talent and train them for elite units? The police department appears to be short on plans to retain or recruit quality and talented staff. Appoint people on merit and on commitment to public service excellence – and combine this with stringent training for those coming from previously disadvantaged backgrounds.

By introducing an army of community police assistants, based in the areas they come from, government will create jobs, undercut poverty and reduce crime. This is the most effective way to restore public confidence in the police and involve the wider community in crime prevention.

Beeld, 20 December 2006

Getting the basics right in the police force

The new muscular police strategy of shoot-to-kill – in an attempt to get a grip on runaway crime – is not the solution. The Criminal Procedure Act as it stands, which Police Commissioner Bheki Cele blames for police inadequacy and wants to amend (with the support of President Jacob Zuma), already gives the police sufficient power to use force if they or the public are in danger – so why do we need a new policy?

The real issues are corruption, inefficiency and a lack of adequate skills and resources in the police service and the criminal justice system. We need a comprehensive turnaround strategy to curb crime, and better policing and an effective criminal justice system must be at the heart of it. The real danger of this new policy is that instead of tackling crime it will encourage trigger-happy policing, as was likely the case in the tragic shooting in Pretoria of Olga Kekana, who was mistaken by the police for a carjacker last Sunday.

Part of any turnaround strategy must involve dealing with the perception that there are individuals who are above prosecution, if they have the right political connections or are aligned with the right political faction within the African National Congress (ANC). Conversely, in some cases people are prosecuted to settle political scores. We must take the politics out of policing, as we must also take business out of policing, asking those with business connections to sever their ties to companies with whom they may be involved.

The police force has a credibility problem, which must be dealt with. There is a public perception that some bad apples are in cahoots with organised crime, if not criminals themselves. Often, almost everybody in a township knows who the criminals are, where the drugs and stolen goods come from and where the gangsters hang out. Yet, the police in many cases appear not to know this or ignore information passed on to them by the public. If the police leadership strategy is to score big wins early on in the fight against crime, the first thing the police must do is to round up the most well-known (by communities) criminal bosses across the country.

There is also a perception that in some instances the police are picking on soft targets, rather than taking on the criminal masterminds. For example, the metro police are often criticised for sitting comfortably on the side of highways and pulling over honest citizens when they should be policing communities where murder, housebreaking and hijackings are commonplace.

The police must get elementary police work right: they must take proper statements, be able to investigate a crime scene properly and should not lose firearms and dockets.

The vacancies in the police force must also be filled, even if it means re-recruiting those who took voluntary retrenchment packages. Cele should go on a drive to attract specialist skills to the police service and expand the recruitment pool, especially to the leadership, to bring the best possible talent on board. He must reinstate the specialised police units, such as the narcotics bureau and the family violence, child protection and sexual offences units.

A police station should be built in every township. This should be done through public works programmes, with the unemployed in the area recruited as labourers. More forensic laboratories are also needed, and more scientists should be recruited, even if means importing from abroad en masse in the interim. Recruit at least 100 000 more police officers, for detective work. Furthermore, recruit another 150 000 matriculants of impeccable character who are unemployed and give them jobs as police assistants in the community.

It is imperative that the police release crime statistics regularly and transparently, so that we can clearly measure progress, and so that civil society, the media and the public can hold the police accountable.

Lastly, as part of a comprehensive anti-crime, poverty and job creation strategy, the government must introduce a basic income grant to help people affected by poverty and the impact of the global financial crisis. This will with one stroke deal with those who are forced to commit crime just to survive, and help focus police resources elsewhere, where it matters most.

Sowetan, 15 October 2009

Not all cultural traditions are worth keeping

The bull that caused recent controversy in South Africa has now been sacrificed in Nongoma – with the approval of the courts. (The sacrifice was part of the *ukweshwama* ritual to offer symbolic thanks for the first crops of the season.)

Yet, the bigger challenge for all communities in South Africa – of whatever colour – remains to honestly re-examine all their cultural, traditional and religious assumptions and practices. It is not going to be easy – these issues go to the heart of our sense of self – but the debate over the killing of the bull offers us the opportunity to re-flect on parts of all cultures in South Africa that may conflict with the values of our Constitution, individual dignity and safety. The judi-ciary may pronounce on cultural practices, but ultimately 'triggers for (cultural) evolution are the people themselves who practise such cultures', as Zizi Kodwa, the spokesperson for President Jacob Zuma, put it.

For instance, as African parents (many white parents also) it was accepted as part of our 'culture' that we would beat a child that mis-behaved. Yet it has been proven that the practice of 'disciplining' a child through beating inculcates a culture of violence.

Our Constitution calls for gender equality. As African males (white South African males also) we have grown up viewing women as our 'possessions'. In the Eastern Cape, king of the AmaMpondomise, Mpondombini Sigcau, criticised the old cultural practice of *ukuthwala* because it was abused – young girls were forced to marry old men. This is the kind of leadership we need now.

Prejudice against gays and lesbians is justified on the basis that it is allegedly against African 'culture' – which is nonsense. Eudy

Simelane, one of the stars of Banyana Banyana, South Africa's national female football squad, was gang-raped and brutally beaten before being stabbed 25 times in the face, chest and legs, because she was lesbian. What kind of culture approves of this?

Many young Xhosa men die every year during circumcision at traditional initiation ceremonies. Firstly, the space must be created for individuals to absent themselves from any traditional ritual he or she opposes – including that of circumcision. Then, the government must ensure better conditions for those who strongly feel the need to participate in initiation ceremonies, like circumcision. Finally, the curriculum for initiation schools should also be adapted to grapple with the new challenges of our time – including the notion of gender equality, safe sexual behaviour and discouraging the dominant 'macho' perception of maleness.

The king of the AbaThembu, Buyelekhaya Dalindyebo, stands accused of kidnapping, arson and culpable homicide. The king is awaiting sentencing after he was found guilty of kidnapping a mother and her six children after he had personally set their home alight, to 'discipline' them. His defence advocate, Terry Price, argued that he should be treated with leniency because of his status.

'What you cannot lose sight of is the fact that he did not go out to destroy lives but was committed to disciplining his community . . . They got the punishment that they deserved,' Price said in mitigation of sentence.

African culture has a long tradition of democratic practices, such as consensus-seeking and internal debates. But it also has some very autocratic practices – it is not wrong to admit this, neither is it wrong to advocate discarding such aspects. Surely, if we claim that our cultural practices allow our traditional leaders to do as they please, then there is something wrong with aspects of such a culture. It is wrong to blindly support morally wrong practices on the basis of cultural solidarity.

Finally, if only those who so zealously defend the most dehumanising aspects of 'culture' would declare the actions of African leaders – their greed, corruption and clinging to power – as being against African culture, and fight these with the same resolve they use to defend these practices, the continent would be a much better place.

Sowetan, 10 December 2009

Is anybody listening?

Government leaders are so staggeringly out of touch with the grim daily reality of South Africa that not even the recent horrifying incidents of xenophobia can jolt them to their senses. After the appalling violence, which has left more than 40 people dead and thousands homeless, leaders, instead of dealing decisively with the crisis and its causes, looked for scapegoats, blaming criminal individuals, rogue elements of the Inkatha Freedom Party (IFP) and a shadowy 'third force' for 'orchestrating' it.

In reality, a deadly cocktail of reasons is to blame for this xenophobic terror.

Firstly, there is a culture of violence at the heart of South African society. Violence is now seen as the normal way – socially, culturally and politically – of dealing with problems. The apartheid state and the liberation movements saw violence as the solution to their var-

168

ious situations and nothing has been done since 1994 to reverse this deadly culture. In fact, in the midst of social and political crises, the democratic government, whether to disable legitimate criticisms or protests, has actually often fallen back on the hardy manual of violence.

Secondly, there is a deep prejudice against 'others', which was reinforced by apartheid segregation. Yet, between blacks there was also an artificial hierarchy, not only between Indians, mixed-race South Africans and Africans on the one hand, but also within these groups, whether it was based on economic status, on one's pigmentation or the size of one's language group. After 1994 foreign blacks were placed at the bottom of this system.

Except for speeches about the rainbow nation there have been few concrete efforts by the government, institutions and civil groups to help people unlearn these prejudices. Given South Africa's history, there will have to be a deliberate strategy to educate citizens on the new civic virtues demanded in our society.

Thirdly, since 1994 community solidarity has almost totally collapsed in black society. Those with an education, political connections to the ANC or who had managed during apartheid to be relatively well off, left the townships for former white suburbs or gated communities, taking with them their business and leadership skills.

This latter group not only dominates the ANC, but also the newly democratic institutions, and benefits from the opportunities opened up by affirmative action and black economic empowerment (BEE). Meanwhile, the townships and informal settlements have been turned into ghettos and those who live there have felt the lack of service delivery the most. They have also little or no access to the ANC, democratic institutions or empowerment opportunities. As a result, more than five million eke out a living in the informal sector.

Yet, this is also where most of the black immigrants have been forced to survive, resulting in a deadly battle for scarce resources.

At the same time, the disadvantaged in the townships have now also reached a point where they want the dividends of democracy: they want jobs, food, access to affordable education, health care, sanitation, electricity, transport and other services. They want their voices to be heard, but so far the government has ignored the voices of this important part of our society. Only last week Finance Minister Trevor Manuel played down the problem of high food prices, saying that South Africa 'is not even among the 50 worst affected countries'.

By blaming scapegoats for the xenophobic violence, the government is again in denial. The economic downturn, the devastating cascading effects of high interest rates and rampant food and fuel inflation, combined with poor delivery of basic services and public corruption, have hit the bedrock of our society the hardest. In places such as Alexandra, perceptions, for some time, have been that black immigrants have the resources to bribe government officials to get houses and licences for taxi routes and trading, while the locals have to stand in never-ending queues. Xenophobic violence is an outlet, albeit a misguided one, for the anger of the masses. If the government remains deaf, we must expect a bigger violent explosion, turned towards other South Africans perceived to be reaping the rewards of the new dispensation.

The Witness, 27 May 2008

Sexist leaders undermine women's rights

Women's Day will be accompanied by the usual turning up of the volume in public rhetoric, as our leaders proclaim their undying commitment to advancing the interests of women. Yet, there is a deep gulf between the call for women's equality in South Africa's model Constitution and society's predominantly archaic attitudes towards women.

More often than not, women are cynically used by the very same male leaders trumpeting gender equality to fill quotas, whether for political ends or to meet the 'broad-based' empowerment criteria required for a black economic empowerment (BEE) contract or government tender. Furthermore, women are being pulled down by cultural, political, economic and religious prejudices that undermine their full participation in society, which in turn deprives both the broader democracy and the economy.

Continuing patriarchy in society means that women lack equality in sexual relationships, the family, the workplace, culture, the economy and politics. Male leaders will have to set an example, something which they have so far failed to do. During the 2004 election campaign, the then president Thabo Mbeki said he would 'klap' (slap) his sister if she was to marry an opposition party leader. And during President Jacob Zuma's trial in 2006, he claimed that he could tell by the way a woman sits or the dress she wears that she is 'looking for sex' and that 'culture' compels him to oblige. Of course, there is no part of African 'culture' – or any other culture, for that matter – allowing for this. In South Africa's Constitution, gender equality overrides culture.

South Africa has a high incidence of violence against women, and sexist views from leaders provide a cloak of legitimacy for such violence. How far we still have to travel can be readily seen in public attitudes about rape. Women are still seen by society and the criminal justice system as responsible for being raped.

African women bore the brunt of colonialism. Colonial and apartheid administrations introduced rigid rules that deprived them of rights in the home and disconnected them from the economy and politics. During the struggle, African women, mothers and wives soaked up the societal ruptures wrought by the dehumanising assaults on the dignity, identity and self-image of blacks.

Often the powerlessness black men felt in the face of the violence of apartheid exploded into violence against women in families, homes and communities. Furthermore, more often than not, manhood, whether in black or white communities, is expressed in macho terms. This is why it is so crucial that political leaders set a progressive example of male (white or black) self-identity that aligns itself with the values of the Constitution.

Alternative and more progressive definitions of male identity must be forged throughout the public school system from the day a child enters school. It should, of course, begin at home. However, the reality is that with the rising numbers of broken families, and the patriarchal views that prevail in society on the role of women, many children are unlikely to get examples of a more rounded male self-identity at home.

There is a real danger that women will again bear the brunt of a seismic geopolitical event, this time the global financial crisis. Furthermore, in the midst of economic decline, feelings of powerlessness in male individuals – who often can see others, more politically connected, but not necessarily better qualified, creaming it, while they remain in poverty – are likely to increase. Self-worth in

South Africa is now depressingly increasingly measured by how much money you have, with those who don't have access to ready streams of revenue seen as lesser individuals.

The ANC adopted a ground-breaking resolution at its national conference in Polokwane in December 2007, compelling the organisation to move to 50% representation for women in all ANC structures as well as in government, parliament and independent democratic institutions. Yet, as Home Affairs Minister Nkosazana Dlamini-Zuma remarked, it was up to the ANC leadership to ensure gender equality was 'put it into practice'. 'The ANC cannot run away from that struggle,' she said. 'It cannot preach the struggle and then not practise what it preaches.'

The 50% principle, if implemented, may perhaps be the single most effective mechanism to transform not only the ANC, but also society. Unfortunately, the Commission for Gender Equality is failing in its constitutional mandate to monitor whether the policy is being adhered to. To succeed, the commission must first take on prejudiced political leaders, rather than deferring to them so as not to rock the boat. The respected economist Amartya Sen argues rightly that 'nothing, arguably, is as important today in the political economy of development as an adequate recognition of political, economic and social participation and leadership of women'.

Sowetan, 6 August 2009

Free press is the key to healthy democracy

The barrage of attacks on the media by politicians the past few months have now become deafening. The media can be irresponsible – a case in point was the public naming of the alleged rape victim in the Zuma trial. It is also true that at times journalists are too chummy with those in power and that some have very lax ethics.

And yes, the race for profits is undermining quality journalism – there are important stories that the media do not cover (as publications have cut newsroom staff, cheap celebrity gossip, gruesome stories and fluffy features verging on advertorial have driven out complex reporting on politics and economics). Very often the level of debate in newspapers is also rather shallow. But to claim that the media, as a group, wants to bring down the government, is against transformation and is targeting particular prominent individuals is ridiculous.

A free press, in combination with an effective parliament and an independent judiciary, is a prerequisite for good governance, and international tribunals and increasingly national ones are clear that politicians and governments may be subject to greater criticism than ordinary private individuals. For example, the European Court of Human Rights has ruled unanimously that because 'freedom of political debate is at the very core of the concept of a democratic society the limits of acceptable criticism are accordingly wider as regards a politician than as regards private individuals'.

It goes further: '[T]he limits of permissible criticism are wider with regard to the government than in relation to a private citizen.' Penalties for defamation in such cases would only apply where the accusations are 'devoid of foundation or formulated in bad faith'.

The seminal judgement in the United States Supreme Court in *New York Times* versus Sullivan (1964) established the principle that there should be greater latitude in criticising a public official, even to the extent of mistaken or inaccurate statements, provided that these were not made maliciously.

Again, according to the European Court of Human Rights, there are two important aspects to the democratic role of the media. One is to inform the public. The other is to act as a watchdog monitoring government. 'It is incumbent on the (press) to impart information and ideas on matters of public interest. Not only does it have the task of imparting such information and ideas: the public also has a right to receive them. Were it otherwise, the press would be unable to play its vital role of "public watchdog".'

The celebrated Indian economist Amartya Sen has shown how a robust press contributes greatly to a democracy. For example, he shows how reporting on the early signs of drought can prevent famines, and how reporting on the nature and the extent of unemployment can force governments to come up with policies to alleviate the chronic effects of joblessness.

So, too, has the media a big role to play in integrating poverty, women and Aids – often neglected – into public policy-making. Enterprising media, using the space provided to them by the democratic system, bring out facts that may be embarrassing to a government – facts that many governments would instinctively try to censor. For example, continued pressure by civil society groups and persistent reporting of the irregularities around the arms deal – even when both the media and civil society activists were frequently vilified by politicians and government officials – led to the successful prosecution of Schabir Shaik.

Sen argues that the absence of effective opposition and the suppression of newspapers give many governments immunity from criticism and political pressure and that this often translates into thoroughly insensitive and callous policies. The Chinese Famine of 1958-1961 killed, it is now estimated, close to 30 million people. The lack of a system for distributing news impartially meant that the Chinese government was misled as to the severity of the situation by local party officials competing for credit in Beijing. In fact, when the famine was moving towards its peak, the Chinese authorities mistakenly believed that they had 100 million more metric tons of grain than they actually did.

Both the media and civil society are crucial to a strong democracy, as model constitutions and transparent official procedures mean little if no one exposes wrongdoing. Often, as Michael Johnston argues: 'Corrupt states abound in inspectors, commissions of inquiry, and recordkeeping requirements that create and conceal corruption rather than reveal it, because no one outside the state can demand meaningful accounting.'

In Brazil, persistent investigation over a two-year period by various media groups, which revealed an influence-peddling ring and high-level corruption within the Fernando Collor government, caused a national uproar and eventually led to the departure of Collor as president.

Often, even if reporting on corruption or other questionable activities does not lead directly to prosecutions, it can lead to the removal of individual politicians or governments at the next available electoral opportunity. In this way, public outrage against official corruption serves as a disincentive. Take the persistent media coverage of the 'cash for questions' scandal in the UK, whereby MPs in the Conservative government of John Major were caught by journalists agreeing to accept cash payments from private parties in return for lobbying for their interests by asking ministers public questions in the House of Commons. The uproar is widely believed to have contributed to Tony Blair's landslide victory over Major in the subsequent parliamentary election of 1997.

Moreover, press reports of corruption can help change a culture of corruption and sleaze in politics. It is better to have a bad press, with pockets of excellence (obviously an all-round quality press would always be preferable), than a cowed or lapdog press.

Sunday Independent, 11 December 2005

Turning black education around

Beyond the usual official rhetoric about black education, one does not get a real sense of crisis. Introducing short cuts, such as downgrading pass marks, is an indication of the lack of seriousness with which the situation is viewed.

There is a link between the rampant anti-intellectualism in the country and the poor matric results. In dominant political circles, knowledge is rarely appreciated. In poorer black communities, education is no longer seen as an escalator out of poverty. Of course, the fact that many black learners see former matriculants wandering the streets, unemployed because they did not graduate with the kind of results that would make them employable, does not help.

No country after the Second World War industrialised without educating the masses. Japan's, South Korea's, Singapore's and now China's prosperity is based on mass education. It is the single most effective BEE strategy, or redistribution tool, and only through education can we reverse the crippling apartheid legacy of deliberate underdevelopment of black communities and lift substantial numbers of people out of poverty.

The continued slide in education entrenches apartheid patterns. A minority in private schools, mostly white, and the children of the small black middle class, can access education that compares with the best in the world. The majority, overwhelmingly black, get the worst education imaginable, leaving them without the skills to navigate the world of work. Without fundamental change in the way education is delivered, blacks will continue to do the menial work, and whites will continue to manage the sophisticated parts of the economy. This is a recipe that has only one outcome – a lack of growth.

But the lack of skilled blacks is not only a drain on the economy; black resentment, anger and powerlessness because of economic marginalisation are a ready time bomb. The election of Jacob Zuma as ANC leader and South African president and Julius Malema as ANC Youth League president shows that anyone, no matter how sparse their education, can make it to the most influential positions in the country. Yet, on the flip side, it also sends out the message that education does not matter. One can advance without education, if one only joins the ANC, becomes a loyal cadre, or links up with a local party boss, and stays loyal to him or her, and so on. And the way in which the ANC's deployment system is currently being manipulated means that even if someone has all the skills necessary (skills gained through an impeccable education), one can be bypassed for a job in the public sector, if not connected to dominant party bosses.

To expect delivery on promises for better education without parents, communities and civil groups keeping the pressure on government and teachers is just silly. As black parents we accept too much mediocrity from our government. Often a township school will be left without windows or a toilet, while the local councillor or politician supposedly representing the constituency drives a R1,2-million car. Those parents that are able to do so must be more involved, not only in tracking the progress of their children, but also in putting greater pressure on government to improve schools.

Good teachers must be rewarded by government, communities and parents, and lazy ones disciplined. It is not the trade union's job to protect poor teachers, just because they are members of the union. In fact, it is the union's job to see that the quality of teachers – its members – is high.

Business must adopt poor schools, instead of appointing token politicians to boards and striking meaningless BEE deals with the politically connected. Government must provide resources to teachers and schools on time – and govern better.

Sowetan, 14 January 2010

What South Africa's women face

Despite the country's progressive Constitution, which firmly entrenches gender equality, South Africa's women face a tough battle. A model constitution, decent laws, and good intentions alone do not end sexism. Popular sentiments must change. For generations, men have viewed women as their possessions. It takes more than laws to fix this.

Recently, former South African deputy president Jacob Zuma was tried for allegedly raping a 31-year-old HIV-positive 'family friend'. He was acquitted in May. At his trial, he told the court that the way the accuser sat and dressed had told him that she was looking for sex. Her knee-length skirt, he said, proved his innocence.

Throughout the rape trial, Zuma's supporters – both men and women – abused the accuser further, going so far as to burn effigies of her outside the courthouse. Few came to her support. The Congress of South African Trade Unions (COSATU) (which has a large female membership) and the South African Communist Party (SACP), both allies of Zuma's, and the ruling ANC, maintained a sphinx-like silence on the rape case. Collectively, their leaderships failed spectacularly to use the Zuma rape trial to help change sexist attitudes. Their silence was deafening.

South African society has always been male-dominated, regardless of race. The recent adoption of our new democratic Constitution challenged the legal system but led to a crisis in male identity that has not been resolved. Men have had difficulty in coming to terms with the changing role of women in post-apartheid South Africa. This tension, I believe, is one of the causes of the rise in violent crime against women.

Gender inequality is at the heart of the Aids pandemic sweeping the country. Because many women have little power in relationships, they are impaired in their ability to exercise control over their sexual lives and the household economy. In the public sphere, leading women are often viewed as adjuncts to their partners, rather than individual politicians in their own right. For example, current South African Deputy President Phumzile Mlambo-Ngcuka is struggling to get rid of the impression that her husband, Bulelani Ngcuka, the former national director of public prosecutions, is the real power behind the throne. Her merits as an astute politician in her own right often appear only in footnotes.

Now, the battle over who should succeed President Thabo Mbeki as leader of the ruling ANC will tell us a lot about the future role of women in South Africa. Mbeki favours a female candidate in part to counteract patriarchal attitudes, but some ANC supporters are suspicious of the idea of a woman president. To them I say: the social costs of sexism are too great to ignore – women face violence and Aids spreads as the rainbow nation's social fabric crumbles. It's strong and smart to promote women's rights in law and in deed.

The Washington Post, 19 December 2006

Turning economic challenges into opportunities

Who stands to gain from nationalisation?

Julius Malema, the outspoken president of the Youth League of South Africa's ruling African National Congress (ANC), may have lost his bid to have his suspension from the party set aside, but the clamour within the ANC for the nationalisation of the country's mines is unlikely to die down.

Malema and the ANC Youth League have become synonymous with the calls for the nationalisation of the mines (in particular), land and banks. Together they have vowed they will oppose the ANC and South African President Jacob Zuma's re-election for a second term at the ANC's 2012 national elective conference unless he supports nationalisation.

Some may argue that now that Malema appears to have been elbowed aside, the calls for nationalisation will die down. To the contrary, many members of the ANC family – including senior members – firmly support it. Promoters of nationalisation, including

183

Malema, appear to have convinced many of South Africa's disenchanted poor – and rank-and-file ANC members – that nationalisation of the mines, banks and land can provide an economic nirvana,
creating jobs and opportunities for all. The appeal of nationalisation is a clear consequence of the failure of the ANC government in
a number of key areas: delivering quality public services to the poor,
slashing poverty, and black economic empowerment (BEE), which
was meant to give blacks a bigger say in the economy.

But calls for nationalisation by some ANC cadres are also based
on the mistaken belief that only the state can deliver jobs, economic growth and wealth, a belief which is augmented by a deep
mistrust of local and international business. Added to this is the fact
that, in the eyes of ordinary black South Africans, the mines are
symbolic of the dispossession of blacks and the enrichment of
whites during colonialism and apartheid.

Almost two decades after the end of apartheid, South Africa still
has stark inequalities and high levels of poverty and unemployment
which run along racial lines. Cyril Ramaphosa, a former general secretary of the ANC, and now a leading black businessman, explains
the new enthusiasm for nationalisation in these words: 'Much as
we understand that poverty and unemployment are rooted in
decades of economic injustice, so too must we accept that the frustration being witnessed today arises in part from our collective
inability to sufficiently transform our economy. This inability has certainly sparked the call for the nationalisation of mines.'

And it is not just the poor: many in the Black Management Forum
(BMF), the Black Lawyers Association (BLA) and the Association of
Black Securities and Investment Professionals (ABSIP) support the
nationalisation call. Together they argue that a state mining company
will give them better opportunities for individual career advance-

ment and will provide procurement opportunities for black-owned companies.

An influential faction within the ANC that can be broadly classified as African nationalists – they want, specifically, black Africans in key positions in government and business – and which includes key figures such as ANC heavyweights Winnie Madikizela-Mandela, Billy Masetlha, the former head of the National Intelligence Agency (NIA), and Tony Yengeni, the head of the ANC's political education school, have also backed the call for nationalisation.

Ironically, both the South African Communist Party (SACP) and the Congress of South African Trade Unions (COSATU) also supported nationalisation before Malema and the ANC Youth League began to call for it. However, in more recent times both these organisations have started to argue for a more nuanced approach, based on a policy of a mix of state and private ownership in the mining sector. This position was outlined by the president of the National Union of Mineworkers (NUM) Senzeni Zokwana, who argued that the trade union view was based on public-private partnerships in the mining sector, similar to those that exist in the diamond-mining sectors of Botswana and Namibia. Governments in these countries mine diamonds in joint public-private ventures with De Beers. Zokwana said: 'You need a private operator because it brings know-how, skills as well as funds.' He then warned that blanket nationalisation, as proposed by the ANC Youth League, could irrevocably damage the South African mining sector and result in thousands of lost jobs.

However, the reality is that COSATU and the SACP's more nuanced standpoint has been eclipsed by the Youth League's populist appeal for outright nationalisation. And in the process the Youth League has appeared as 'more' pro-poor than COSATU and the SACP, the two organisations within the ANC alliance that have projected

185

themselves supposedly as the 'vanguard' of those fighting to better the lives of the most impoverished South Africans.

Meanwhile, ANC General Secretary Gwede Mantashe has said that the issue should not be about nationalisation versus privatisation, but about how to create a mixed economy. Zuma has also privately told business leaders that nationalisation is neither ANC nor government policy. But since the president himself has not clearly stated as much in public, an awkward policy vacuum exists around the issue.

South Africa's business leaders have so far responded badly to the calls for nationalisation. The initial reaction of the mining sector and organised business was to issue strongly worded statements to the effect that privatisation was bad, 'socialist' and 'communist'. This played right into the hands of the ANC Youth League, who portrayed business as 'opposed' to 'transformation', and as being 'unable' to provide alternatives to tackle black poverty.

South African business must accept it is not blameless. Many companies have implemented BEE and affirmative action by appointing politically connected individuals to boards and senior executive positions in the hope that they will provide political 'insurance' against calls for radical redistribution. Other more cynical companies are criticised for appointing token blacks who are then set up to fail – which allows the companies in question to argue that affirmative action isn't working.

The nationalisation debate will be finalised at the ANC's 2012 national elective conference. It is likely that selective nationalisation will be accepted as the way forward: property already in private hands will not be nationalised, but unexploited resources will be. We are also likely to see mining regulations being tightened and the current state-owned mining company given more powers.

Ultimately, South Africa already has a huge nationalised sector, but it is wasteful, often led by incompetent political appointees and rarely delivers effective services. Managing existing state-owned companies and all spheres of government more effectively, more honestly and more accountably, and governing in the interests of all rather than in those of a small elite, are more effective solutions to our current problems than nationalisation.

Rapport, 9 February 2012

Beat the recession by fighting it together

The greatest economic downturn since the Great Depression of the 1930s presents obvious dangers but it also offers South Africa a rare second opportunity to refashion its economy so that it finally lifts more people out of mass poverty. However, to grasp the opportunity we will have to be innovative. Equally, we must act with urgency.

Sadly, it took confirmation of the news last week that South Africa has plunged into recession for the first time in almost two decades to shake government, business and labour leaders out of their complacency. In his first state of the nation address today, President Jacob Zuma must outline an immediate stimulus package which must point to a shift in both fiscal and monetary policy. This is a crisis, so there has to be more flexibility with inflation targeting: lifting the upper bands surely cannot be imprudent. The Reserve

Bank must also cut interest rates more aggressively as part of the package to cushion the blow to the most vulnerable and to kick-start the economy.

The time has now arrived for Zuma to start making really tough decisions. The first must be to tackle greedy bankers, who are strangling the economy with their selfish behaviour. This recession will deliver a double whammy of misery. It will hit the middle classes, both black and white. But the poor will be hit the hardest.

This is the moment to introduce a basic income grant to support poor families with school-going children up to the age of eighteen. There also has to be a formal intervention to put a lid on soaring food prices. And, finally, there must be a ceiling on price increases by state-owned companies such as Eskom, Telkom and Metrorail.

The reality in this tough downturn is that the private sector is unlikely to be able to create jobs en masse. It will have to do that in conjunction with the public sector. Many companies can be rescued by their involvement as partners in a massive public works programme to build infrastructure. In all these public works there should be an insistence that only local products be used. The public works programme must be rolled out more creatively to catch up with the backlog in black areas.

Black economic empowerment must be scrapped in its entirety or at least be restricted to one person for each BEE deal. Transferring more than R500 billion to a dozen black oligarchs, purely on the basis of their political connectivity, is scandalous.

Trade unions must now also become more creative. This is not the time to insist on wage increases of 15%, as the National Union of Mineworkers did. They should consider job sharing, working half-time, taking a cut in salaries, to keep as many people as possible in jobs. And company managers, whether in the public or private sector, must forego bonuses and take salary cuts.

Sowetan, 3 June 2009

Small farmers too often forgotten

The extraordinary rise in food prices underscores the importance of having effective land reform and agricultural strategies. Government should focus on getting a large number of poor people to grow their own food so they can at least feed themselves.

The rapid industrialisation of all of the successful East Asian economic tigers was preceded by sweeping, but effective, land reforms. South Africa will have to create a balance between encouraging competitive commercial farming and developing small farmers, who can at least provide for themselves and their surrounding community.

So far, ANC leaders have encouraged the creation of black commercial farmers, just as they have encouraged the establishment of BEE tycoons. Meanwhile, ordinary farmers have been neglected in the same way small, micro and medium businesses (SMMEs) have been neglected – close to five million people are eking out a living in the informal sector, whether selling peanuts on the roadside or running a spaza shop. The real entrepreneurs, who will starve unless they sell their wares, have been thrown under the proverbial bus while the black oligarchs created by the government, former politicians turned businessmen or big commercial farmers, have

189

accessed most of the R200 billion given to promote BEE over the past decade.

If just a fraction of that money had been transferred to the authentic entrepreneurs, who have created and run SMMEs, redistribution would not only have been more broad-based and poverty reduced much more significantly, but economic growth would have been higher, and more jobs would likely have been created. The same neglect of ordinary black farmers has also meant that millions who could have at least fed themselves now go hungry, because they do not have access to land, microfinance and training.

South Korea, one of the most successful of the East Asian tigers, started off at the end of the Second World War, like South Africa, as a country where land distribution was among the most unequal in the world. Then 80% of the rural population was landless and 3% of those living in the countryside controlled 60% of the land. Yet, the efficient redistribution of land saw almost half of the land equitably redistributed over a period of only two years (between 1948 and 1950).

Perhaps one reason why land reform has not been very successful so far is because South Africa does not have an organised national civil movement specifically focused on securing equitable land reform, but that should not stop the government from giving poor families small plots of land so that they can at least start providing food for themselves. Households headed by women should also be specifically targeted.

The redistribution of land must naturally be closely linked to a training programme that teaches people not only how to farm most effectively but also how to manage their businesses. The aim must be to ensure that small farmers produce food.

South Africa should dust off the cooperative systems used so effectively by Afrikaner farmers. In this way, small farmers can pool their products, marketing strategies and finance-raising abilities. Whole rural communities, *dorpies* and villages can set themselves up as farming cooperatives, with every family in the area having a share in the concern. This will be true broad-based empowerment.

Furthermore, the shortage of food across the globe presents opportunities for South Africa's commercial farmers. The kinds of produce needed most in local and world markets should be identified and production focused on them. Lucrative niche markets – such as organic produce – should also be identified.

The global food crisis, which is likely to continue for some time, presents the same economic opportunities as the current commodities boom. It will be a shame if South Africa fails to turn the food crisis into a boon, but taking advantage of it requires an effectively coordinated broader industrial policy that aims to transform every sector of the economy by implementing new economic development initiatives.

The Witness, 1 May 2008

Offer a new social pact

The global financial crisis offers developing countries such as South Africa the opportunity not only to refashion their own economies, but to help create a new global financial system. But they will need a plan.

The coordination of macroeconomic policy across countries is crucial. Developing countries must have a greater say at the International Monetary Fund (IMF), World Bank, United Nations (UN) and other global bodies. They must push for emergency aid for poorer countries that does not come with the IMF's inappropriate conditions. They must insist on more freedom to come up with their own economic policies.

There must be better regulation of financial institutions, limits on executive pay and punishment for those responsible for the crisis, as well as the restructuring of credit-rating companies. They failed to pick up the United States' subprime trouble. Yet they wield enormous power over developing countries.

China has unveiled a stimulus package of four trillion yuan ($586 billion) to boost domestic economic growth. It will be spent on infrastructure development. France unveiled a 26 billion-euro plan, focusing on boosting investment in infrastructure, skills and technology transfer.

Countries such as South Africa don't have the means for these packages. Yet, with a smaller budget, South Africa can still be innovative.

Any stimulus package must consist of fiscal and monetary measures. South Africa is already spending R400 billion on infrastructure development. The downturn must be used to expand low-cost housing stock and employ the unskilled and unemployed on a mass scale in a combined programme of public works and skills development.

We could turn the army of unemployed into plumbers, electricians and bricklayers, while building the five million houses needed, plus dealing with infrastructure shortages in townships, informal settlements and rural areas.

Tax breaks could be given to companies making new investments, creating jobs, using local products and generating new technology. By expanding the budget deficit by at least 1% over a restricted period a stimulus package could be financed to create jobs and boost investment and entrepreneurship, with income support to the most vulnerable.

BEE must be scrapped in its entirety or restricted to a single individual or BEE company per deal. Where BEE companies are supported, it must be on the basis that they are creating jobs, transferring skills, developing new technology and expanding the local manufacturing industry.

This is also the moment to come up finally with a plan to rid the country of its dependency on exporting raw materials, so that the economy is not so dependent on the vagaries of world commodity prices.

Strategic industries such as agriculture must be supported. Homeowners must also be protected – government and banks must find a way for those in trouble to renegotiate their home loans.

The financial crisis means that skilled South Africans abroad may have more of an incentive to return home and government should lure them into the failing public service.

Government waste, corruption and inefficiencies will have to be dealt with head-on. We cannot waste precious resources. Labour and business must work together to solve this crisis.

Developing countries must together find a collective mechanism to stabilise their currencies to avoid free fall in the financial crisis. They must also introduce tough measures to punish currency speculators. There has to be more flexibility on inflation targeting, lifting the upper band by a percentage point and extending the period, say two years, to reach it. The Reserve Bank must cut interest rates.

Tackling this crisis could be the basis of a new social pact between government, business and organised labour – a pact crucial to remaking the economy.

Mail & Guardian, 15 December 2008

Take the ideology out of land reform

Land reform cannot continue in its current form. Yet if land reform is not dealt with in a responsible and sensitive way by government and interest groups, enormous damage can be done to race relationships in South Africa. Not only that: the principle of security of tenure will be disturbed and commercial agriculture could potentially be destroyed, leaving many destitute and the country without food security.

It is imperative that land reform and a more inclusive agricultural sector are achieved. If not, peaceful co-existence between historically advantaged whites and historically dispossessed blacks will remain elusive. Currently, the debate around land reform is mostly confined to populist public calls from some senior ANC leaders to change the Constitution to give government the right to expropriate land without reimbursing farmers, or inflammatory statements, such as those by Freedom Front Plus leader Pieter Mulder that 'Bantu-speaking' people have no historical claim to 40% of the country's land.

It seems as if official land policy deliberations are happening in the smoke-filled backrooms of a small group within the ANC party leadership – leaving many other stakeholders in the dark, and either fearful or angry. Land reform should take place in an environment where all the stakeholders in agriculture have been consulted: farmers, businesses, organised labour, civil society and government. They must come together in a CODESA of sorts, where they should agree to a social pact which will outline a new agreement with time frames for land reform.

South Africa cannot afford land reform policies which are driven by ideology. Instead, these policies must be pragmatic and innovative. Land reform should be integrated into broader long-term economic and infrastructure development strategies, as well as industrial and manufacturing policies. This is currently not the case. Most importantly, the success of land reform should not be measured by numbers, that is, by the percentage of land transferred from white to black hands. It should rather focus on how effectively recipients of land are able to use it in a sustainable and productive way.

A key aspect of land reform should be to safeguard the sustainability and expansion of the commercial agricultural sector. The country should be able to provide for its own needs and must remain competitive in the global market, with the ability to earn handsomely from agricultural exports. Agricultural output must be increased significantly while jobs are created and a sustainable livelihood is provided for people in rural areas. This can only be done if the principle of land tenure security is safeguarded. Furthermore, other options rather than the wholesale transfer of commercial farms should be explored. These could include giving shareholding to farm workers and providing tax breaks to farmers who transfer skills to workers.

The truth is that not all dispossessed landowners, or their descendants, necessarily have an appetite or an inclination for farming.

195

Redistribution could come in many different forms, one being a Brazilian-style basic income grant for families linked to recipients keeping their children in school, and those without children contributing a day's community service.

Available state land in rural areas could also be transferred to poor communities or rural families to enable them to grow their own food. Communities can run such land as a cooperative and they can receive basic agricultural training. Therefore an audit of the land that government owns is urgently required. Communal land – which is often run by chiefs as their personal fiefdom – should be reformed in conjunction with this, since it will most probably be put to better use by emerging black farmers.

It is a shame that land is often transferred to black economic empowerment tycoons who use it as a trophy, rather than making it productive. Instead of giving land to well-connected individuals or politicians with no agricultural background, small-scale or emerging farmers should be identified. It is also crucial that emerging farmers receive the necessary support in the form of access to finance and training. Some poor communities have had to sell the land they received – in a few instances to the very farmer from whom it was bought – because they just do not have the required background in farming.

Where existing commercial farms are redistributed, a condition should be that these farms are managed commercially on behalf of the recipients or in partnership with them. A pillar of land reform should be to bring emerging farmers into the supply chains of larger private and public companies.

The statement by Agriculture, Forestry and Fisheries Minister, Tina Joemat-Pettersson, that white commercial farmers may have to look for opportunities elsewhere on the continent does not contribute anything to the land reform issue. In South Africa every skill is important, no matter what the colour of one's skin is. Land reform policies should be aimed at retaining every white commercial farmer who wants to farm. We should not be exporting them to other countries, whether as mentors or as farmers. As with other tricky policy issues, in the end successful land reform will require constructive partnerships between all the interested parties.

Rapport, 22 April 2012

Be wary of the Chinese dragon

South Africa's willingness to bend over backwards to appease China is undermining our hard-fought struggle for democratic gains. It also allows the Chinese dragon to buy up strategic sectors of the South African economy, which will only lead to a new form of colonialism – this time not by Western powers, but by the East.

It appears there are expectations within government that China may become a big financier of South Africa's R850 billion infrastructure roll-out. It would be detrimental to look only to China for financial backing and not to seek financiers from a large spectrum of emerging markets and the old industrial powers. The hard truth is that capitulating to China will bring few new benefits and only make us prisoners of China's whims. South Africa's best strategy should be to play China off against other emerging markets, the industrial powers in the West and to dramatically expand its trade with the rest of Africa.

China's hardnosed strategy has been to portray itself as different to the West in its dealing with Africa, supposedly more fair, more developmentally orientated and more altruistic. But don't be fooled. China's involvement in Africa, including South Africa, has nothing to with charity and a need to help: it wants raw materials and land access to the continent's markets. In short, it wants to make money from Africa.

Of course, there is no doubt that China should be a key geopolitical ally for South Africa. After all, a pillar of our foreign policy strategy is to make the structure of global trade, economics and politics – currently staked against African and developing countries in favour of Western economies – fairer. China and other emerging markets' increasing power have already made many multi-lateral agencies scramble to incorporate the interests of developing countries which were previously mostly ignored. Many developing and African countries have already been able to extract better terms on deals from industrial powers. They have done so by using the potential of a booming China, as well as other emerging powers as alternative trade partners, as a bargaining chip.

Diversifying the markets for South Africa's products is also a key strategic foreign policy goal. The strategy of diversifying trading partners should be about more trade with a whole new spectrum of emerging markets, such as Brazil, India, Russia, South Korea, Turkey and the rest of Africa. It broadens the narrow focus on the country's traditional trade partners in the European Union and North America.

Some South Africans, including sections of mainstream business, opposition parties and a number of think tanks, oppose the idea that the country should have strategic political and economic alliances with China. Many who hold this view argue that South Africa's strategic alliances should remain with the industrial West – North

America, Australasia and Europe. Europe is currently still our largest export market. Many activists on the left of the tripartite alliance also totally reject South Africa embracing China as a geopolitical and economically.

Last year South Africans were outraged when Janice Linden, a 38-year-old black South African, was executed by legal injection after she was found in possession of 3kg of methamphetamine at Guangzhou airport in China in 2008. President Jacob Zuma tried but failed to secure a stay of execution. South Africa's impotence in its efforts to persuade a supposedly close ally sparked anger across the country. It made many question why South Africa goes out of its way to accommodate China politically, while the Chinese are not willing to reciprocate.

Home Affairs Director-General Mkuseli Apleni admitted that South Africa feared a 'backlash' from China similar to those experienced by France and Australia after they allowed the Dalai Lama to visit their countries. Yet the Dalai Lama visited emerging markets in Mexico and Brazil without any political or economic consequences.

Some leaders within the tripartite alliance uncritically admire the Chinese model of development without democracy. They usually still embrace Soviet-style socialism and claim that China's dizzying economic growth rates 'proves' their thesis that democratic niceties are an obstacle to development and public service delivery. Many in this group also argue that the Constitution is an obstacle to development. The Chinese have been taking senior ANC leaders on regular 'workshops' to China, where the more impressionable are lectured on the Chinese way of pursuing economic development without democracy.

Currently, the trade deficit between China and South Africa is skewed in favour of China. South Africa exports cheap raw materials to China (which does not create jobs), while China exports labour-intensive manufactured and beneficiated products (which does create jobs). While Chinese products can easily enter the South African economy, local products face a mountain of hurdles in China. The ANC government has come under intense scrutiny by allies and opponents for not aggressively up-scaling its strategy of beneficiating South African minerals; and for not being pro-active enough in boosting and protecting South Africa's manufacturing sector.

South Africa should tax the exports of raw materials heavily, especially those being exported to China, if we are serious about beneficiation. Alarmingly, China is also buying into strategic sectors in the South African economy, such as platinum, rare metals and the financial sector – which should drive South Africa's economic development.

Several South African executives of state-owned and private companies have pointed out how Chinese companies are making inroads into Africa, in the process outmanoeuvring South African companies, whether private or state-owned. They have asked for active government support for their investment drives into the continent, claiming that Chinese companies have an unfair advantage because they are, in effect, subsidised by the Chinese state.

Chinese state subsidies also affect the local textile industry since the South African government does not give the same direct and indirect subsidies that the Chinese give theirs. In 2006, after lobbying by industry, trade unions and ANC members, the South African government persuaded China to sign a textile pact between the two countries which would limit imports from China and give the local industry a window period to rebuild itself. South Africa could have introduced tougher protective measures, like the WTO-endorsed measures implemented by the US and EU.

According to Etienne Vlok, a textile industry analyst, China agreed to a watered-down bilateral textile pact because it feared that South Africa would copy the US and EU and implement much harsher protective steps. In 2009, though, China refused to renew the textile pact, despite the fact that the government was in the process of blocking a trip by the Dalai Lama to the country in an effort to show its loyalty to China.

South Africa's ferrochrome producers have also been calling for government support to stay ahead of their Chinese counterparts. The Chinese government is subsidising various raw material imports, including chromium, as part of fostering beneficiation strategy. China imposes a 40% export duty on metallurgical coke – the sole ingredient South African ferrochrome producers import, mostly from China. Frans Baleni, the general secretary of the National Union of Mineworkers, says the Chinese are also stockpiling chrome and ferrochrome in order to dictate prices in the future.

Furthermore, Chinese companies actively buy shares in local mining companies and seem to be concentrating on strategic minerals and struggling black miners involved in these sectors. BEE deals in the mining sector have often been financed by mining companies lending black buyers the money to purchase the stakes. However, many of these deals have unravelled as the black part owners could never finance the debts through dividend payments. Many of these black miners are now hoping Chinese companies could buy into them.

The government should be more proactive in identifying the sectors in which Chinese and other companies should invest, as part of integrated long-term economic and infrastructure development plans. Sadly, though, the general pattern of Chinese investments in Africa appears to be that the Chinese decide what and where they invest in a particular African country, mimicking the colonial and Cold War investment and aid-driven economic patterns, which brought economic growth with little industrialisation or broad-based development.

It would be good to remember that China needs South Africa and Africa's raw materials to keep up its current growth. China needs to export its products to African markets and feed its hungry with food from the continent. The moment economic growth slacks in China, North African-style revolt against the one-party state could become a reality there. China's long-term stability is not neces-sarily certain and South Africa should therefore not hedge all its bets on China.

China also needs South Africa as a strategic political ally – not only against the hostile West, but also to secure the friendships of other African and developing countries with which South Africa has strategic relations. Moreover, the EU is still the biggest buyer of South African products: any rapid change that will make China the new market for most products currently exported to industrial na-tions are going to be very costly to the local economy.

To deal with an economic giant like China, tiny South Africa will have to box smarter in its dealings with that country. South Africa should make better use of the resources available to us in the pub-lic and private sector, as well as in civil society, to negotiate better deals with China. A partnership must be forged between govern-ment, business, labour and civil society to come up with competitive strategies. South African companies, such as Sappi and SABMiller, have done incredibly well in China and other emerging markets:

their capacity must be leveraged to come up with better long-term strategies in that country.

Lastly, South Africa has the largest indigenous Chinese diaspora community in Africa: it is a tragic waste that the government is not using the skills of these South Africans to help plan the most strategic approach towards China.

Sunday Independent, 6 May 2012

Squandering our skills

In a fiercely competitive world the top-performing countries are those that are able to produce cutting-edge skilled people and keep them, if not lure them from elsewhere. Investing in human capital, which includes building an educated workforce, is one of the main reasons for the success of the East Asian tiger economies.

The phenomenal growth of emerging economies over the past few years, and the old industrial nations' scurrying to respond, has put a further premium on human capital. But this is also partly what the success of countries like the United States and Britain has been built on for the past century – their ability to be a magnet for skills from all over the world.

There is a huge shortage of skilled professionals around the world because countries are not able to produce enough skilled people. Industrial nations are poaching scarce-skilled workers from developing countries in order to stay competitive. Developing countries that are misruled, undemocratic or indifferent to local talent

203

make it easier for their skilled professionals to be recruited from abroad. For managers, politicians and leaders in South Africa to expect a magic wand of 'patriotism' to prevent skilled people from taking up overseas offers is foolish.

Secondly, to think that South Africa could 'manage quite well, thank you', when it loses skilled people to other countries is to misunderstand what makes some countries excel and others remain in the lower divisions. Of course, many talented people will always want to broaden their horizons, skills and experience by studying or working abroad. And many will return with more skills.

In a world where scarce skills are crucial to a country's success, its most talented citizens must be encouraged to return. Foreigners with scarce skills must also be actively recruited to work in South Africa in the same way that talented South Africans seek opportunities abroad.

Last month the captain of the South African netball team, Bronwyn Bock-Jonathan, left for Australia, after being recruited to coach the AIS Canberra Darters and the Netball Academy. Bock-Jonathan has a PhD in sport science, having researched how sport can improve the lives of teenage girls on the impoverished Cape Flats, and has lectured in sport science at Stellenbosch University. She has also captained South Africa at the netball world championships at senior and under-21 level.

Bock-Jonathan has unique skills and the lack of response from local netball, sport and even political leadership to retain people like her sums up South Africa's cavalier attitude towards its most talented people. Such an attitude will not only cost the economy dearly, it will also impoverish South African society.

Early this year, the top management of the South African military warned that the rate at which soldiers, sailors, pilots and technicians were being poached from the South African National Defence Force from abroad posed a serious threat to the country's security. In June, apparently, ten senior South African Air Force technicians resigned in one week after being recruited by an Australian aviation agency. This after twenty aircraft engineers were recruited the month before.

South African Airways (SAA) is in the process of voluntary retrenchment to get rid of 225 pilots, as a cost-cutting exercise to try to reach its target of making a R1,7-billion profit. Airlines such as Emirates and Qatar are lapping up the highly trained South African pilots. But SAA's short-sightedness is typical of South African public institutions. It would have made more sense to cut down on the excessive bonuses of SAA's non-performing CEO Khaya Ngqula.

For developing and African countries to be competitive, competent political leadership is also a scarce skill that may be more crucial than in industrial nations. The problem of most struggling African and developing countries is not that they don't have competent political leaders, it is that these leaders are often blocked from reaching the top because of the way the political system is structured.

Most African and developing countries cannot get out of this political leadership trap; they have the available leadership skills, but the structurally imposed restrictions keep them out and reward the mediocre. In South Africa the ANC is tearing itself apart over Jacob Zuma who may be a very decent person, but who is not going to give South Africa the cutting-edge political leadership that this country now so desperately needs to remain competitive. The uncertainty his ascendancy into the South African presidency will create may actually push local talent, of whatever colour, away.

It is perhaps even more scandalous that political circumstances increasingly appear to make Zuma the ANC's shoo-in for the country's presidency when the ANC itself abounds with skilled leaders.

The Witness, 29 July 2008

Luring skilled workers to our shores

Just the other day the Australian government announced plans to recruit 20 000 skilled professionals across a number of fields from abroad. Many East Asian countries have long used targeted foreign recruitment to shore up industries where there are skills shortages. This is the route that South Africa should take as a matter of urgency.

Recently, President Thabo Mbeki stated that he would consider recruiting skills from abroad to boost the ailing local government sector. Indeed, Mbeki and senior cabinet members increasingly blame an acute skills shortage for hampering service delivery and for being a brake on reaching the magical 6% economic growth rate. Not surprisingly, many, like Labour Minister Membathisi Mdladlana, instinctively baulk at recruiting from outside. They are wrong, though.

Government should immediately set a target of say 100 000 professionals, in the sectors in which South Africa is most desperate for skills, to recruit within a specific time frame. It is clear that the rapid expansion of the economy has outpaced the production of skilled workers, and the public education system, neglected over the past decade, is just not going to churn out the skills the economy needs.

Even worse, the economy is also losing skills, either through migration or the underuse of existing skilled workers – both white and black. Australia also loses a lot of its most skilled employees to other countries, especially to the United Kingdom, where Australians occupy senior positions in most industries. However, the Australian government has obviously accepted that in a highly globalised world a country is always going to lose some skills, even if there are incentives for skilled workers to remain local, and is seeking to redress their current shortage. Some of the most industrious and entrepreneurial people are always going to seek work or study experiences abroad. The key challenge for government is to secure the return of at least some of those leaving temporarily and fill the gaps left by those who do not return.

South Africa falls far short of providing even the most basic incentives to skilled citizens to remain in the country or return after a temporary stint abroad. It should now be obvious that South Africa must speedily embark on an organised mass recruitment drive, rather than a piecemeal voluntary one, to lure skilled workers to our shores. The young and industrious, as well as 'old' skills from other countries, must be given the opportunity to seek out South Africa as an experience abroad.

Obviously, local business will have to start doing their bit to develop skills. For example, the fashion by local companies of poaching black talent from one another by luring them with more money is just short-sighted. Would it not make more sense to recruit people young, or even better, to identify talent at school level, fund their studies and thereafter train them through the business chain? Beneficiaries of such a recruitment method are likely to exhibit far more loyalty than workers who are simply plucked from another company.

In both London and New York, companies spend a lot of money bringing young people in as interns, especially in the financial services sectors. There is a myth that to enter the economic sectors or the financial sectors a degree in these areas is a must, but the reality is that people with a more general education can be mentored to make a career in almost any specialised sector – as they do in London and New York. This is particularly relevant in South Africa where there are a large number of unemployed black graduates, most of whom have a general, rather than a specialised tertiary qualification. If companies had in 1994, or earlier, recruited black talent en masse as they entered universities or at school level, we could now have had a formidable new generation of South African middle managers. Local businesses must start to train employees in this way as soon as possible.

Government must also do its part – its efforts to transform the education sector have been truly appalling so far. Just remember the disaster of offering the best teachers voluntary severance packages. Furthermore, instead of wasting money on creating black tycoons – who often do not enlarge the economy – invest in the education system. This makes more sense in a modern economy where human resource advantage gives an economy the competitive edge. In addition, there has to be an extensive effort to make all existing domestic skills productive – both white and black. Black skills cannot be excluded from government because they have the 'wrong' politics or opinions, or are not politically connected. White skills must be brought back into the system, by re-employing those who are willing to train or mentor others.

Finally, South Africa has a competitive advantage over most emerging economies, in that it is attractive to skilled foreigners – but we are not using it.

Sunday Independent, 12 September 2005

Consumers fighting for their own interests

The increase in bread prices, implemented by all the main producers at about the same time, cannot be a coincidence. On Monday, Tiger Brands increased the price of a loaf of bread by 40 cents. The other big companies, Pioneer Foods and Premier Foods, say that they will also increase bread prices.

These increases are particularly galling, given that the main bread producers are currently under investigation for price fixing. Last year Tiger Brands were fined R99 million by the Competition Commission. The other big producers – Pioneer Foods, Sasko, Food Corp's Sunbake and Premier's Blue Ribbon – were given immunity.

The bread price increase is a clear case for the Competition Commission to investigate whether any collusion has taken place between the big bread producers to artificially set the price of bread. There are certainly enough grounds now for the Competition Commission to launch an investigation into the whole milling, storage and baking value chain. The series of increases in interest rates, the price of basic foods and electricity have South Africans, especially the poor, reeling. Yet, so far, the regulators have not decisively investigated these increases.

Last year, the National Electricity Regulator gave Eskom the green light to increase electricity prices by 14,2%. Both Eskom's and Telkom's prices are so high and their services so below par that it has become a national pastime to complain about them. Their high tariffs also impact negatively on economic growth. It took the public protector until this week to start murmuring that perhaps it should probe Eskom about the reasons behind the perpetual electricity outages.

The public protector's constitutional mandate is to police public institutions that prejudice any individual. Surely, poor service from state institutions and parastatals falls under this category?

Similarly, the interest rate hikes by the Reserve Bank cause hardship and restrict economic growth. Most other central banks around the world take note of the general economic conditions and try to ease conditions when it appears that monetary policy is unduly stifling growth. Yet, in our case, the mandarins at the Reserve Bank appear hard of hearing.

One immediate impact of the deep divisions between government and the African National Congress (ANC) is that if there has been policy paralysis in the government over service delivery in the past, this is now likely to worsen. It is unlikely that there will be any decisive central government action to cushion the negative impact of, for instance, increases in the prices of basic foodstuffs, as the central government and the ANC square off against each other.

Public watchdog institutions will now have to assert themselves and take leadership roles to protect ordinary South Africans. Sadly, the record of most audit and watchdog agencies in protecting citizens has been very poor. In the past, most of them have deferred to the executive or have been soft on unscrupulous business organisations. A case in point is the fact that large companies still get away with destroying the environment. The Competition Commission's fining of Tiger Brands for price fixing last year was a welcome break from the depressing norm of inaction by public watchdogs.

A big failing of South Africa's young democracy is that so few organisations are set up specifically to protect consumers. Without consumer watchdogs, such as patients' protection organisations to monitor hospital services, bank consumer organisations to check indiscriminate repossession of defaulters' homes or commuters' organisations to protest about poor public transport, the democratic system cannot work properly. Of course, it is not the place of the government to start these organisations. Consumers, i.e. ordinary citizens, will have to take the responsibility.

During apartheid, selected consumer organisations fought against unscrupulous businesses, and civic organisations played an important role in selectively fighting on behalf of consumers. However, these civics are either not around any more or, as in the case of the South African National Civic Organisation (SANCO), have lost the plot.

South Africans will have to develop a large number of consumer organisations which are not afraid to flex their muscles. One contemporary example of effective citizens' organisations is the ratepayers' organisations. Without such organisations, our democracy is much poorer.

The Witness, 19 January 2008

Overcoming Africa's democracy deficit

A blueprint for change

There cannot be any clearer illustration of the impotence of Africa's continental and regional institutions than their inaction in the face of the wave of popular rebellions against dictators in North Africa. They were silent when popular rebellions kicked out autocratic leaders in Tunisia and Egypt and they have been equally clueless in dealing with the crisis in Libya – the African Union (AU) mission was a massive failure and in the absence of leadership from Africa, the United Nations (UN) and other powers stepped in to try and resolve the Libyan and other African crises.

African institutions and leaders also failed spectacularly to deal with the situation in Côte d'Ivoire, where former strongman Laurent Gbagbo refused to step down after losing presidential elections to Alassane Ouattara. Again, the failure of African leaders and continental institutions in Côte d'Ivoire meant that a former colonial power, France, played a key role in mobilising international pressure to force Gbagbo to step down.

Africa's subregional institutions have been equally impotent. The Economic Community of West African States (ECOWAS) had one emergency meeting after another, but got nowhere close to resolving the Côte d'Ivoire crisis. The Southern African Development Community (SADC) has yet to stop Zimbabwean autocrat Robert Mugabe's tyranny. In fact, during crucial moments, SADC and regional leaders have actually reinforced Mugabe's power. Similarly, in Swaziland, King Mswati has battered his people, but still receives the red-carpet treatment from SADC.

The AU, the home-grown continental structure set up to find African solutions to local problems, has not done any better in either of these countries and it has failed spectacularly in other African hotspots, too. It has fallen far short in trying to broker an end to the bloody conflict in the Darfur region of Sudan. It has also failed to come up with a workable plan to deal with inflation or come to grips with the crippling food and fuel shortages that plague many countries on the continent – issues which are at least in part due to bad local leadership, mismanagement and lack of democracy. A common response to other regional problems, such as the HIV/Aids crisis or the devastating impact of the global financial crisis, has also been lacking. Not surprisingly, African countries worst hit by food shortages – including Zimbabwe, Egypt, Cameroon, Gabon and Ethiopia – are also among those with the most autocratic governments, and where the AU's silence has been the most deafening.

For all the rhetoric of 'African unity', AU member states have rarely voted together in international forums to safeguard common African interests. The 'unity' record of regional institutions, such as SADC and ECOWAS, is similarly compromised. Individual African countries are usually bought off by former colonial powers – continental and regional institutions have had no mutually beneficial policy for interacting with other nations or economic blocs. The only unity found has been when dictators have clubbed together behind the AU, SADC or ECOWAS to shield each other from criticism by ordinary Africans, civil groups or outsiders when battering their citizens.

For example, Africa has been divided on how to respond to the European Union's (EU's) economic partnership agreements (EPAs), with some countries rejecting them and others embracing them. EPAs force African countries not to trade with countries or regions competing with the EU. A common response from African continental and regional institutions would have made it difficult for the EU to punish those refusing to sign up and prevented them from playing African countries off against each other.

It is now a truism that Africa's future prosperity in an increasingly uncertain, complex and rapidly changing world depends on building even closer political and economic ties between countries on the continent. African countries now desperately need the stability, the security and the independence to make policies freely that only a continental 'pooling of resources and cooperation' can provide. Unfortunately, the current regional and continental institutions are too discredited, too toothless and the rules for membership too lenient. The solution is to radically overhaul these structures. In order to reverse this dispiriting situation, African countries will have to bring new energy and ideas to make these institutions work for them. Furthermore, we need new objectives and new concepts (and even new words) that are appropriate for our times. The ways in which many African leaders and institutions generally think about closer integration is outdated. The idea of a Pan-Africanism, in which all African countries become one big, happy family, is unworkable, unachievable and simply silly. To continue with these ideas will

215

mean that Africa is unlikely to reach its full potential in this generation and become as prosperous as, say, the East Asian tigers.

The current wave of rebellions against dictators that started in North Africa, the global financial crisis and the rise of emerging economies such as China, Brazil and India – the combination of which is likely to remake the world – offer a critical juncture for African countries to pursue comprehensive reform of continental and regional institutions. In fact, given the rupture that the global financial crisis is causing, the continent may end up poorer, unless it changes direction.

African political unity must be selective. A revamped AU must begin with a small group of countries that can pass a double 'stress' test based on the quality of their democracy and the prudence of their economic governance. When the final decision was made on the structure of the AU in 2001, there were two options on the table to determine membership criteria. One option argued for selective membership based on meeting certain democratic and developmental criteria. The second option argued for all African countries to be members. This latter option was pushed by some of Africa's 'big men', including Libya's Gaddafi and Zimbabwe's Mugabe. Clearly, this was a lost opportunity.

The AU has, in fact, no entry requirements. Because membership of the AU is largely voluntary, countries like Zimbabwe can still be members, even if their governments have appalling human rights records and continue to spectacularly mismanage their countries' economies. This means that Zimbabwe and all the other rogue regimes in Africa can be fully-fledged voting members, determining the outcomes of crucial decisions within the organisation.

In fact, the AU should start as a three-track system. There should be a core group of countries that meet the minimum democratic and economic governance criteria. A second group should be made up of those that did not make the cut in democratic and economic management terms, but which are serious about pursuing the new objectives of the AU. This group should be assessed on an annual basis to see whether they are ready to enter the core group of countries. The rest, the third group of countries, would be the various dictatorships – which should be shunned until they introduce democratic governance.

By compelling members to follow a set of good economic and social policies, the citizens of African countries who are outside this new AU will have a clear set of standards against which they can measure their own governments' performance – which will allow them to put pressure on their governments to deliver.

Of course, there are not many African countries that will pass such a test right now. Stricter rules will mean that the AU will start off initially as a small club of countries. At best, perhaps only South Africa, Mauritius, Botswana, Cape Verde, Namibia – and then only if the criteria are in some cases flexibly applied! Nevertheless, the countries which pass the test for acceptance into the elite tier should harmonise economic policies and standards of democratic governance. These top-tier African countries could create the first Africa-wide set of industrial policies and put in place a long-term economic development strategy aimed at lifting African countries up the industrial value chain.

Once this has been done, every country must then set developmental targets, say for five years. At the heart of these plans for development must be for African countries to diversify, from raw materials to beneficiated products. As former UN secretary-general Kofi Annan rightly said recently, 'Africa is overreliant on unprocessed commodities'. This, coupled with insufficient investment in

217

manufacturing and infrastructure, means that old patterns of trade are being replicated with new partners, such as China and India. Without some kind of intervention it is unlikely that African governments will be able to translate this situation into widespread job creation, poverty reduction and economic prosperity.

Countries which adhere to the democratic and economic management criteria should be rewarded with new investment, development funding and support. Special Africa investment funds should be set up – for example, pooling the proceeds from sales of commodities – to finance infrastructure across the continent. Proceeds from such funds would then be distributed on the basis of the willingness of nations to reform, and targeted at underdeveloped areas of the countries that meet the criteria.

The AU core countries would then adopt joint positions on foreign policy, and act as a bloc in multilateral organisations with regard to international treaties and on common issues, such as climate change. The AU could also directly negotiate with, say, China when trade deals are struck, to safeguard the interests of individual countries.

Peace and security policies in Africa have had, as under the Organisation of African Unity (OAU), state security as their focus, rather than human security. This wrong-headed principle is at the heart of the shielding of despots such as Zimbabwe's Robert Mugabe from criticism, rather than coming to the aid of their desperate citizens. For the OAU, African presidents were more important than the continent's people. This has remained unchanged under the new AU and regional institutions.

Another obstruction has been that African leaders always side with each other when they are criticised by the West, especially former colonial powers, no matter the merits of the criticism. This must stop. African solidarity must not be based on leaders backing each other blindly, but on values, such as democracy, social justice, clean government, ethnic inclusiveness and peace, protecting ordinary Africans against disease, violence and hunger, and prudently managing economies for the benefit of the continent's people. To achieve this, African countries will need to cede some of their sovereignty. The AU's charter will have to be changed from protecting the sovereignty of individual countries to protecting the security of Africans themselves. The African principle of non-interference in the affairs of neighbours still partially informs the AU, which has been very reluctant to intervene forcefully in misgoverned nations.

Social and economic integration, caused by globalisation's adjuncts of urbanisation and the free flow of information, means that borders are increasingly meaningless. There are no 'national' crises in Africa any more: a crisis in one African country will quickly turn into a crisis in the whole region, eventually affecting the whole continent. Zimbabwe's problems are South Africa's – as the three million destitute Zimbabweans that fled chaos in their country for a better life in South Africa attest. Similarly, in East Africa, if Kenya catches a fever, so too do Uganda, Tanzania, Rwanda, Burundi and the Democratic Republic of Congo (DRC).

There is little provision for ordinary African citizens to have any kind of influence on AU and regional institutions' decisions. Historically, African leaders have been very reluctant to have anyone, let alone their voting citizens, influence their institutions' policies. So far, these institutions have been glorified clubs, mostly for dictators. Measures should be introduced to allow ordinary citizens and civil groups to vote on crucial policies of continental and regional institutions.

A revamped AU (and revamped regional institutions) could play an important role in constructing a new democratic political culture

219

across the continent. Importantly, the fact that most African countries are so ethnically, linguistically and culturally diverse means that democracy and inclusive development must be the glue of any nation-building process. Many African countries have still not reformed the limited democratic institutions and restrictive laws inherited from colonial days. In many other countries where democratic institutions, such as parliaments and human rights commissions, have been set up, these often exist in name only. This must change – member countries of revamped AU and regional institutions will have to establish credible democratic institutions: an independent judiciary, electoral commissions and human rights bodies.

Part of the revamp must include the establishment of effective Pan-African institutions, such as a continental supreme court and a constitutional court. These courts should be independent and have jurisdiction over member states, so that when tyrants like Mugabe emerge they can no longer depend on the acquiescence or support of fellow rogues. These institutions must be able to compel members to scrap all repressive laws. Most African countries, just like Zimbabwe, have 'insult laws' that outlaw criticism of the president – the secretary-general of Zimbabwe's opposition Movement for Democratic Change (MDC), Tendai Biti, was prosecuted under these laws. Yet the AU does not demand from its members to repeal such oppressive laws. Once again, this must change.

Political parties in AU member countries that receive state funding should adhere to basic democratic rules. This will prevent one-man parties and tribal parties. The AU must also set new minimum standards of conduct for both ruling and opposition parties. Most of them are undemocratic, corrupt and tribally based – they cannot lead the continent to a new era of quality democracy and prudent economic management. In addition, every member country will have to adhere to a limit of two terms for presidents, and there will have to be a transparent procedure to impeach presidents or leaders who start off as democrats but turn into tyrants, so that we do not end up with the likes of Mugabe again.

Africa urgently needs an 'inclusive and forward-looking' democratic and economic development plan. Political and economic integration on a continental level, if done seriously, may perhaps be the thing that will lift Africa out of decline. But the African integration project must be genuinely democratic, giving ordinary citizens a real say in decisions that will ultimately impact on their lives. The debate about the future of the continent must not be limited to leaders or the elite – as is the case currently.

Post-independence Pan-Africanism failed to secure a sense of ownership when it came to African integration projects – it was top-down, leadership-focused, exclusive and non-participatory. The current efforts of the AU and regional institutions are very much in danger of falling into the same trap. These institutions must now urgently be reformed, to close the continent's gaping democracy gap and create enduring stability and equitable growth.

Open Space magazine, 27 July 2011

Africans inherited corruption

Most well-intentioned, corruption-busting remedies in Africa fail because the root causes are often poorly understood. Post-independence African countries inherited deeply corrupt institutions from previous colonial and apartheid governments. Instead of changing them for the better, African governments have – on gaining independence – almost always further entrenched these deeply compromised governance systems.

In most African colonies, the colonial elite centralised political, economic and civic power. The institutions that should serve as watchdogs against corruption in any society – the judiciary, police and security services – also served only this elite and were often subservient to the all-powerful colonial administrator or governor. Meanwhile, the colonial private sector, producing in most cases for export to the 'home' market, was usually deeply dependent on the colonial government and so rarely held it accountable.

At independence the African colonial elite were often replaced by another narrow elite, this time the independence movement's aristocracy – the dominant independence leader and dominant 'struggle' families, or the dominant ethnic group or political faction. African independence movements are often highly centralised or strongly dominated by a single leader and his political, ethnic or regional faction. The dominant structural make-up of these movements means that they fit seamlessly into a centralised political culture, much like that of a colonial government.

The newly acquired state bureaucracy – military, judicial, nationalised private sector – was often seen as the 'spoils' of the independence struggle and many struggle aristocracies dished out patronage – jobs, government tenders and newly nationalised private companies – to their political allies, ethnic group or region. Obviously, this meant that the idea of merit-based appointments was thrown out of the window – even if the newly empowered independence movement launched economic development programmes to transform the colonial economy, such reforms were

hardly going to have any impact with unqualified cronies managing key public institutions.

Very few African countries had a significant private sector at independence. Those that did more often than not saw it nationalised,
partly because the grass-roots cadres of independence movements
expected to be given jobs after the struggle.

In some instances liberation movement governments embarked
on a policy of creating a 'capitalist class' of new 'indigenous' business owners. In many such instances political capital formed the
basis of these attempts at creating indigenous capitalists: those
closely connected to the government received either stakes in newly
privatised public companies, state tenders to supply services for the
government or slices of private companies owned by former colo-
nials, minority groups or foreign businesses. Of course, those who
benefited from these programmes are hardly the ones to bring
governments to account if they fail to uplift the majority of the
population economically.

Before independence, the small colonial elite often lived lives
of conspicuous consumption – expensive mansions, high-profile
shopping trips in the capital of the mother country, lavish parties.
A culture of hard work was often absent. Sadly, many of the post-
independence African elite – of both the politically and economically empowered class – took the colonial elite's conspicuous consumption as the mark of 'success'. Not surprisingly, some of the poor
also want to emulate this 'bling' lifestyle – and may not see any
problem with leaders living like this, even if they themselves remain poor.

In the struggle for liberation, progressive civil groups usually
joined the liberation as part of an anti-colonial alliance. At independence most liberation movements argued that civil society had

now played its historic role and should be 'demobilised', or the leaders of these groups were incorporated in some way into the governing party. Compounding this lack of authoritative critical voices is the fact that in some African countries the main opposition parties are either associated with the colonial or white-minority government, or opposed independence.

During their struggle, independence movements were by nature secretive. They often had to use subterfuge to foil the secret police of the colonial or white-minority government. Sadly, because of this, most have governed with obsessive secrecy once they achieved power, which encourages corruption.

Liberation and independence leaders were often put on a pedestal by supporters. This idolisation, more often than not, continued after independence – allowing leaders to get away with corrupt practices. Historically, most leaders in Africa have lacked the political will to genuinely tackle corruption, but this must change. Ruling parties must bring a new calibre of leadership forward at all levels – competent, honest and decent. A system of merit must be brought into the internal party elections. Africans need to actively encourage new kinds of leaders, with a new value system – not solely based on struggle credentials.

The colonial legal system – which was often blatantly unjust – forced many among the oppressed to find ways to escape laws and rules. Unless independence leaders in the post-colonial period set clear examples in following the rule of law, the masses continued such practices. Ruling parties in Africa today should punish the bad behaviour of their leaders and members – legally, if it is justified – and reward good behaviour. Only if this is done publicly will governments restore the moral authority to deal credibly with transgressions from ordinary citizens.

Finally, there needs to be more exposure of corruption by African media. At present, public officials often dismiss international organisations' corruption reports on Africa by saying that these reports are infused with Western bias, which overlooks corruption in Western countries and focuses on developing nations. Of course, this is true to some extent. However, that should be a separate debate and should not downplay the real, serious issue of corruption at home. Blaming the legacy of colonialism and apartheid – although certainly with us – has become an easy answer for not acting against corruption. This will have to change.

Sunday Independent, 19 March 2012

Wanted: capable leaders for Herculean challenges

In poor countries, competent political leadership is a scarce skill that matters even more than in industrial nations. Industrial nations, where power is dispersed across the society, can tolerate bad leaders better. Better still, bad leaders can generally be voted out.

Since independence, African leaders have usually come to power when their countries are in great crisis – which demands extraordinarily capable leadership. Most African leaders have had to – amidst great expectations from long-suffering citizens – unite ethnically diverse societies, where one group was often advantaged by the departing colonial powers, and equitably transform poor economies.

They must also build lasting democracies by creating new institutions. And while doing this, they must steer their countries through hostile global political minefields. Take the example of South Africa. Our country is stuck in a number of interlocking crises: broken communities; an HIV/Aids pandemic that has been neglected; soaring poverty, unemployment and crime; a pervasive air of public corruption; rising racial animosity; battered democratic institutions; rapidly declining public confidence in government's ability to deliver services; and looming economic problems ahead.

South Africa is also struggling with the consequences of one-parent and child-headed families. We need progressive responses on how to foster stable families, how to make gender equality – as set out in the Constitution – real, how to set an example of male identity that conforms with the values of the Constitution and how to involve men in child rearing. The country must deal with these problems in an increasingly complex, dangerous and economically volatile world.

To deal with these issues a national leader will need new ideas, direction and energy. But the country also needs leadership that can mobilise diverse talent across the ethnic, ideological and political divide. With all these problems, the leadership must in all instances act in the widest possible interest of all of South Africa, not only a small component thereof.

But we also need honest leaders. On their own, any of these challenges are difficult enough – combined, they are a Herculean task that demand that African countries secure special leaders that can guide their countries through these multiple crises. The right kind of leader in fractious, ethnically diverse and underdeveloped African countries can be a rallying force that helps binds them together, and helps unleash the country's productive energies.

In contrast, a bad leader, in the context of fragile democratic institutions, ethnic diversity and underdevelopment, can be terribly destructive – holding back democracy, growth and nation-building. Worse, in African countries bad leaders are difficult to get rid of, and remain a drain on the system long after they are eventually gone.

To respond to these challenges, many citizens of African countries rightly demand 'strong' leaders. But 'strong' leadership is often confused with militancy, tough political rhetoric and silky oratory. Leaders that shone in opposition in the struggle for liberation and independence, where tough rhetoric and militancy were often necessary to counter the brutality of colonial powers or white-minority governments, may not be the kind of leaders needed to reconstruct a crisis-ridden post-independence African society.

Most African countries cannot get out of a political leadership trap – members of political movements, citizens and interest groups often want a tough-talking leader, even if he (mostly he) has no competency when it comes to the majority of the challenges faced by the country in question.

The problem in most African countries is that there is a mismatch between the kind of leaders pushed forward by political movements and the kind of leaders these countries really need to tackle their enormous challenges.

Sowetan, 26 November 2009

A glimpse of African tigers

A shipment of weapons from China destined for Zimbabwe's Robert Mugabe is an obvious trigger for the West to denounce Beijing's involvement in Africa. But Western business and political leaders have long been watching China's re-engagement with the continent with trepidation.

China is setting up Confucius schools, laying out roads and railways and stitching together deals to buy commodities – oil, platinum, gold and minerals. Perhaps not since the first wave of independence during the late 1950s has there been such a buzz in Africa. And crisis meetings, conferences and summits are being hurriedly put together as the United States (US), the EU and Japan scratch their collective heads over how to respond.

China's investment may offer Africa the first real chance to lift itself out of poverty, not unlike post-war Europe under the Marshall Plan or the industrialisation of the Asian tiger economies, neither of which could have happened without US investment. Between 1945 and 1978, the US poured the equivalent of all the aid given to Africa into just one country, South Korea. This is the kind of commitment Africa needs.

The response to China's interest exposes Western hypocrisy and perhaps betrays a sense that African countries are still considered colonial possessions. While the US, France and the United Kingdom (UK) have slashed or dubiously inflated aid figures, China is promising to double assistance to Africa by 2009. Western development aid is still mostly used to push donors' commercial interests, rather than poverty alleviation; much Chinese aid to Africa is likewise tied to business deals.

But China is widening access to its markets for African products –

something Western governments have been reluctant to do – and has offered aid without onerous conditions.

China's involvement is not all positive, as the support given to Mugabe's regime shows. Its model of one dominant political party that quashes dissent is inspiring a number of African leaders just as the continent is seeing a proliferation of opposition parties and a mushrooming of civil movements. But African autocrats have also been helped by the US war on terror, which has allowed them to round up and imprison critics without fear of international condemnation.

International nongovernmental organisations (NGOs) and governments, including African ones, must tackle China's unwillingness to use its leverage with Sudan to end the conflict that has killed or displaced millions. But, at the same time, we must not lose sight of the fact that the countries of most of Africa's longest-serving leaders – Togo, Gabon, Equatorial Guinea, Angola, Cameroon, Mauritania, Guinea, Uganda and Swaziland – either have oil, or are partners in US anti-terror campaigns. Neither situation is acceptable.

Western firms' dodgy investments in Africa are still a political blind spot. African governments must not make the same mistake with China – they should insist that trade pacts with China include clauses committing it to respect labour rights and the environment. China needs the resources of the veld just as much as Africa needs its money.

To continue its 9% growth rate, China's economy requires a mass of resources that can only be found in the necessary quantities in Africa.

But to make the partnership work for them, African nations will have to be more hard-nosed. China is buying strategic assets cheaply and with few obligations. Africa must ensure that partnership deals boost its shrinking manufacturing industry and quickly diversify its economies. It must not squander its riches again.

The Guardian, 24 April 2008

Africa's version of democracy is in deadly crisis

Unless African ruling elites overcome their obsession that regular elections – where the winner takes all – is the main measure of democracy, the orgy of violence, such as that over disputed elections in Kenya, will be repeated elsewhere on the continent.

Western donors, with their requirements that elections are enough to warrant aid, have helped along this limited view of democracy. Zimbabwe is staging its long-awaited presidential elections this weekend, with Robert Mugabe's ruling ZANU-PF so blatantly rigging the elections that the outcome risks the same terrible violence.

Because of this narrow view of democracy, very few African governments put much effort into building relevant democratic institutions. The separation of powers, such as an independent judiciary and a system of checks and balances between branches of government, exists largely on paper. Furthermore, the idea that there are limits to power, which need to be enforced, is mostly a foreign concept.

In Kenya, for example, President Mwai Kibaki appoints electoral commission officers and the judges that hear electoral petitions –

mostly ones aligned to him. In Zimbabwe, Robert Mugabe is directly manipulating the commission overseeing the country's coming
elections.

Most African countries have adopted winner-takes-all electoral
systems, ones ill-suited for such ethnically diverse societies. Winners of African elections often gain access to state power and to
pork-barrel land, business and jobs for ethnic supporters. Losers
are almost never accommodated. In fact, they are brutalised into
submission, with opposition figures all too frequently jailed on
trumped-up charges. Many African independence and liberation
movements, now ruling governments, saw their movements as the
embodiment of the nation or the 'people', with the leader or founder
the tribune of the 'people'. In this scheme of things, opposition parties are seen as the enemy, to be annihilated at all costs.

Some African leaders think they and their movements have the
divine right to rule forever, because they 'delivered' liberation – not-
withstanding their poor records in power. Jacob Zuma has said that
the ANC will 'rule until kingdom come'. Robert Mugabe, Zimbabwe's
leader since independence in 1980, has vowed that the country's
main opposition party will never rule during his lifetime.

Africa's high-stake winner-takes-all electoral systems, and the
damaging consequences for the losing party, often combined with
ethnically based competition, make for a deadly and toxic cocktail.
Unless Kenya and other African countries adopt permanent power-
sharing arrangements that give electoral losers a stake in the political system, punish parties campaigning on ethnic lines and reward
pluralistic ones, the orgies of electoral violence seen in Kenya will
be endlessly repeated.

Most African countries are a hotchpotch of ethnic groups and
languages. Diverse ethnic groups make building democracy more

difficult, but not impossible. Yet most African political parties are dominated by the same ethnic group, and campaign on blood and clan grounds rather than policies or issues.

Very few African leaders turn their countries' diversity into strength. Instead, while preaching Pan-Africanism and blaming the West for colonialism and imperialism, they have been quick to play the tribal card. Most African opposition parties also organise along tribal lines. They often appear to exist solely to oppose the sitting president or government, rather than providing an alternative vision of government with clear policies to match. In Zimbabwe, with the ruling strongman Robert Mugabe for the first time looking vulnerable ahead of the 29 March poll, the main opposition Movement for Democratic Change (MDC) is split into two, mostly because of the brittle egos of its two leading figures, the old stalwart Morgan Tsvangirai and the Young Turk, Arthur Mutambara. The result: a weakened Mugabe may just scrape through because of a divided opposition.

In Kenya, a deal has now been stitched together to douse the ethnic flames which saw more than 1 500 killed and close to a million displaced. President Mwai Kibaki's ruling Party of National Unity (PNU) and opposition leader Raila Odinga's Orange Democratic Movement (ODM) will share power, with Mr Kibaki as president and Mr Odinga as prime minister. African countries will do well to learn from this deal.

The Independent, 26 March 2008

Africa's Frankenstein

What turned Zimbabwe's dictator Robert Mugabe into such a monster?

Firstly, Mugabe, like many other liberation leaders, has been unable to step away from the violence of the liberation struggle. ZANU-PF leaders fought to oust the colonial powers, but they also used violent measures – assassinations, terrible torture and degrading imprisonment – against their own comrades, when they were perceived as too critical or seen as internal rivals. Such actions were often done under the pretext that the victims were spies or agents of colonial powers or whites.

When ZANU-PF came to power, the violence of the independence struggle continued with, if anything, increasing intensity. In the early 1980s, for example, around 20 000 critics of Mugabe were slaughtered in the Matabeleland massacre. Members and supporters of ZANU-PF said nothing about these initial excesses. Firstly, because they did not want to give ammunition to Britain and white Rhodesians, with which they could hammer the new government. Secondly, because they knew action against those who criticised the government would be swift, and their careers and businesses were often completely dependent on the continued patronage of the ruling party. Thus, a culture of silence was born.

In the case of Zimbabwe, even Western nations were initially soft on Mugabe because they desperately wanted the new government to be a success. Activists from other liberation movements, including South Africans, who witnessed the increasingly intolerant behaviour of Mugabe and those close to him, also kept quiet because they too did not want to be seen to be providing Zimbabwe's critics with ammunition or undermining a fellow liberation leader.

233

Mugabe early on assumed the trappings and attitudes of a 'supreme leader' – something the lack of criticism, both internal and external, allowed him to do. As soon as he assumed power, Mugabe purged ZANU-PF of all potential rivals and appointed trusted loyalists in key positions. He then distributed patronage to the chiefs and in return sought control – through them – of their subjects in the rural areas. He also extended his hold on key churches and their leaders. He quickly lost his sense of humanity and every violent act appeared to numb his capacity to feel for victims still further – the supporting masses became little more than numbers, instead of flesh-and-blood individuals.

Initially, local civil groups deferred to Mugabe and ZANU-PF. Appointees to independent watchdog, audit and oversight institutions, because they were mostly appointed from the ranks of approved party members, did the same. The media was nationalised and editors appointed who practised uncritical 'sunshine' journalism, while allowing themselves to be used to destroy the reputations of perceived critics of government. Ordinary citizens kept their heads low – to survive.

Most African leaders argue that because they and their movements led the struggle against colonialism, only they have the 'right' to rule. This is why fellow African leaders have almost invariably shied away from publicly criticising Mugabe. The idea that any opposition, whether from within or outside, is legitimate is a totally foreign concept to most of them. The liberation movement is the people.

Mugabe lives in a bubble where he only listens to his inner circle and neighbouring liberation leaders. This is why criticisms of Mugabe from regional African leaders are so crucial. However, when – in the SADC crisis meeting that discussed the Zimbabwean elections – new Botswana president Ian Khama, from a totally different generation, insisted Mugabe be publicly reprimanded, his older peers resisted. Perhaps only a total generational change will alter this.

Beeld (column also appeared in *The Witness*), 6 May 2008

Africa: How we killed our dreams of freedom

We cannot continue to blame the past. Across the continent, liberation movements that fought against colonial rule have failed to sustain democratic governance. The great Tunisian writer Albert Memmi noted this phenomenon as far back as 1957. In *The Coloniser and the Colonised*, he wrote of the tendency of liberation movements, once in power, to mimic the brutality and callousness of former regimes.

In recent years, Zimbabwe's ZANU-PF has become the symbol of the descent of African liberation movements into brutal dictatorship, but backsliding liberation movements in Algeria, Angola, Ghana, Kenya, Namibia and other countries have left in their wake the lost hopes and shattered dreams of millions.

In the inner sanctum of South Africa's ruling ANC they have coined a word for it: 'Zanufication'. As Zimbabweans flee across the border to avoid police brutality or the hardships caused by an economy in free fall (inflation at more than 1 700% and shortages of basic foodstuff), they whisper it in hushed tones, a warning.

235

A senior national executive member of the ANC, Blade Nzimande, warned recently: 'We must study closely what is happening in Zimbabwe, because if we don't, we may find features in our situation pointing to a similar development.'

Unions, sections within civil society and church groups daily inveigh against the South African government's head-in-the-sand policy towards Zimbabwe and President Thabo Mbeki's 'quiet' diplomacy. COSATU has complained to the South African Broadcasting Corporation (SABC), the public broadcaster, over its failure to cover the Zimbabwean meltdown. But despite this, and although the ANC in South Africa and ZANU-PF are light years apart, the spectre of 'Zanufication' haunts South Africa, raising the question: Is there something inherent in the political culture of liberation movements that makes it difficult for them to sustain democratic platforms?

The irony is that it is often the heroic leaders of former liberation movements who have become the stumbling blocks to building a political culture based on good governance on the African continent. The former South African president Nelson Mandela and President Thabo Mbeki enthusiastically proclaimed in 1994 that the end of official apartheid was the dawn of a new era. Yet many liberation movement leaders – Mugabe is a good example – still blame colonialism for the mismanagement and corruption on their watch.

Obviously, the legacy of slavery and colonialism, and now the challenges of globalisation, are barriers to development. However, to blame the West for Zimbabwe's recent problems is not reasonable. Yet South Africa's quiet diplomacy, from which most African countries take their cue, is based on this assumption. Initially ANC leaders also bought into this idea, but thankfully, on Zimbabwe, Mbeki is increasingly isolated – though true to his contrarian and stubborn nature he still argues that because Zimbabwe was given a raw deal by the British, Mugabe's regime should not be criticised publicly.

In terms of land, black Zimbabweans did indeed receive a raw deal, but that is not the whole story. The Zimbabwean government was idle for at least a decade and when it finally did implement a land reform programme, this consisted of giving fertile land to government cronies who subsequently left it fallow.

The story is similar elsewhere on the continent. As African liberation movements came to power their supporters were keen to overlook shortcomings. The feeling was that a new, democratically elected government needed to be given an extended chance. In South Africa, for example, criticism of the ANC by supporters has always been muted. 'You cannot criticise yourself,' an ANC veteran once admonished me.

There has also been a fear that criticising the government gives ammunition to powerful opponents. When a top ANC leader, Chris Nissen, broke rank and publicly criticised a party official's errant behaviour, he was warned: 'Do not wash the family's dirty linen in public.'

As a journalist – active in the liberation struggle – I, too, gave in to this principle in the heady days after South Africa's first nonracial democratic election in 1994: 'Let's not criticise too much; let's give the new government a fighting chance.' But that was a grave mistake. All governments must be kept on their toes.

The problem for most liberation movements is how to establish a democratic culture. During a liberation struggle, decision-making is necessarily left in the hands of a few. Dissent and criticism is not allowed lest it expose divisions within the movement, which could be exploited by the colonial enemy. But if this culture continues during the first crucial years of power, it becomes entrenched, making criticism at a later date almost impossible. Especially when, as in many African countries – with South Africa the exception – the state is virtually the only employer after liberation and patronage can be used to reward or sideline individuals.

In Africa, in the early liberation years, governments have often operated as if under siege. Take, for example, the South African government's initial inaction on the Aids pandemic. Mbeki embarked on a fatal policy of denial. Many ANC supporters knew he was wrong but kept quiet, in case they were seen as supporting Western governments or big pharmaceutical companies bent on perpetuating Africa's current state of underdevelopment. Many activists preferred to keep their misgivings about government policy to themselves, rather than be placed in the camp of the 'neocolonialists'.

In Zimbabwe, Mugabe brutally quashed rebellions in the 1980s, killing thousands in the Matabeleland region. No regional liberation movement said anything about it. This silence laid the foundations for his reign of terror.

Even the idea of an opposition – internal or external – is a difficult concept for many. Mugabe's ZANU coerced the Patriotic Front (PF), the other major liberation movement in Zimbabwe, to merge with it in the 1980s, hence the name ZANU-PF. This eliminated a possible opposition force.

The resurgence of an opposition is due partly to a generational change in the country's politics. Many of the MDC's supporters are young – the articulate MDC spokesman Nelson Chamisa, for instance, is not yet 30 years old – and have experienced ZANU-PF mainly as a party in government that exploits its people. They are not impressed by past liberation credentials.

In South Africa, it is young activists in the Treatment Action Campaign and their leader Zackie Achmat who have been responsible

for forcing the government to adopt more responsible Aids policies. Zwelinzima Vavi, leader of COSATU, says: 'We are not prepared
to be merely "yes-leader" workers' desks.'

The sad truth, however, is that waiting for another generation
before there can be real change is costly, even deadly, for ordinary
Africans, not least Zimbabweans.

New Statesman, 2 April 2007

Building African 'tiger' economies

Saving Africa's free trade area from failure

In June 2011 African leaders unveiled concrete plans to create an Africa-wide free trade area, announcing that 26 African nations will join the three existing regional trade blocs. Their ambition is to create the duty- and quota-free movement of goods, services and businesspeople by 2016, and an Africa-wide economic and monetary area by 2025.

There are very obvious advantages to an African free trade area. Pooling their markets may help African economies take better advantage of new growth opportunities offered by the rise of powerful new powers. It may also help African economies overcome new challenges caused by the decline of some of the old industrial powers in the aftermath of the global financial crisis.

Given the debt crises in the United States (US) and the European Union (EU), it becomes even more important for African countries to integrate speedily. Currently, African countries trade more with the rest of the world, mostly their former colonial powers, than with each other, and better intraregional trade can provide a protective buffer from global shocks. Furthermore, many African economies are so tiny that they cannot compete on their own. An Africa-wide free trade area will bring larger economies of scale and better access to markets, which in turn can, potentially, expand production and demand.

What should be done differently to prevent the idea of a grand African free trade area turning into a grand failure? The first requirement is political will – at the heart of many African development failures.

There are a number of regional trade blocs in Africa, all with different rules and regulations, and all at different stages of integration – all of which could slow the building of a free trade area. Whatever the level of integration within these regional groupings, all of them have struggled to free the movement of goods, labour and services. Protectionism is rife in African states, and restrictive trade permit requirements and frequent bans on imports from neighbours persist. Non-trade 'tariffs' such as travel restrictions, poor physical infrastructure, incompetent public administrations, rampant corruption and political instability are also major stumbling blocks.

Economic disparities between African countries present further obstacles. Smaller countries fear domination by bigger neighbours, while bigger ones fear that a grand free trade area would lead to domination by South Africa.

Africa's recent growth has mostly been because of a boost in mineral exports, increased demand at home, due to growing domestic markets fuelled by a rising African middle class, and increased trade with new emerging powers, such as China, India and Brazil. Former United Nations (UN) secretary-general Kofi Annan rightly calls this African growth spurt 'low-quality' growth. Not only because it is based almost entirely on exporting raw materials – there has been little attempt made to diversify into manufacturing, services and value-added products – but also because the growth has remained 'inequitable, jobless, (and) volatile' and has not led to widespread job creation and poverty reduction.

A report by the Economic Commission for Africa (ECA) and the African Union (AU) released in July 2011, titled 'Economic Report on Africa 2011', urged Africans to diversify production and exports through improving 'competitiveness by tackling supply side constraints as well as improving infrastructure and productive capacities, among other things'.

The challenge is for individual African countries within a grand free trade area to specialise: one country must produce what another country can't, but needs. In fact, each African country should pick the manufacturing and service sectors in which they may have competitive advantages, and then trade or barter with each other. At the moment, if one African country needs a manufactured product, few neighbours can provide it. Each African country should be required to draw up an industrial policy which should have the goal of diversifying from one agricultural product or commodity to value-added products at its heart.

All the individual industrial policies must feed into a regional industrial policy, which in turn should be connected to a continental industrial policy for Africa. The existing regional blocs should be turned into regional economic growth zones. Infrastructure – power, transport, telecommunication networks and so on – should be developed within each country, within and between the regional economic growth zones. A continental infrastructure grid must connect the regional economic growth zones.

Up to this day most infrastructure networks in most African countries have not changed since colonialism. Colonial powers mainly constructed infrastructure networks in the countries under their control from the small areas that produced the one commodity or agricultural product to the coast for export to the 'mother' country. They rarely connected neighbouring countries. Sadly, African countries during the post-colonial period have left such infrastructure arrangements untouched and even unmaintained.

The bulk of the indigenous sectors of most African economies are in the informal sector, and this is also where most of the jobs are being created. A free trade zone among Africans will be useless unless it includes small traders in the informal sectors, who often face formidable bureaucratic barriers.

All the regional blocs must work towards macroeconomic convergence – setting basic prudent standards for fiscal and monetary policy. Exchange rate volatility – often because of poor monetary policies – has been a particular problem in Africa.

Convergence of macroeconomic policies will be a challenge, given the history of African countries overemphasising political and economic sovereignty. Most African countries have trade agreements with former colonial powers, which often undermine integration with other African countries. And under the US African Growth and Opportunity Act (AGOA), the US signs trade arrangements with individual African countries – rather than with regional blocs. This undermines African regional integration and the formation of regional supply chains.

It would be naive to think that emerging powers such as China and India will suddenly open their markets to African products. In reality it is very difficult for products manufactured in Africa to penetrate these markets, and given the impact of the global financial crisis, it is unlikely that high tariff barriers and subsidies in either industrial nations or the emerging powers are going to decline significantly – in many cases they may become more protective and cut development aid. But even if countries did suddenly lift tariff barriers and cut subsidies, many African producers would still be unable to compete. When it comes to manufacturing and services, most African countries simply cannot compete. However, though African produce and services may be uncompetitive internationally, African countries can trade these products and services with one another, if they can of course bring down the costs of transportation between nations and do away with red tape and corruption.

The big challenge for Africans is going to be to set out a legally binding mechanism – and penalties – to get signatories to the free trade area to stay the course. More effective ways of resolving disputes between members must also be found, as it is inevitable that these will occur.

Lastly, better African leadership and greater democracy remains a crucial barrier in creating an effective free trade area. African citizens – farmers, traders and civil society in general – must actively participate in building a grand free trade area, if it is to be durable.

BBC Focus on Africa magazine, October-December 2011

Africa should follow the West's example, not its advice

Western countries more often than not do exactly the opposite of what they tell African countries to do. For instance, they are now bailing out commercial banks and strategic industries with public money. Yet they discourage African countries from doing the same.

Global financial institutions, such as the World Bank and the International Monetary Fund (IMF), while instructing developing nations to pursue mostly irrelevant, if not destructive, policies, are silent when industrial nations do exactly the opposite. African countries must stay away from these international organisations – if it is absolutely necessary to borrow, they must do so from other sources.

The success of the East Asian states since the Second World War has much to do with ignoring the advice of the World Bank, the IMF and leading Western nations. Instead, they actually followed exactly what Western nations did to grow their economies. Meanwhile, African countries slavishly followed what they were told by the West and former Soviet bloc and Chinese communists, rather than studying carefully what these countries actually did.

Most African countries since independence, while pursuing foreign investment, as suggested by Western nations and global financial institutions, sold off state-owned assets cheaply. They made it easy for global companies based in their countries to repatriate their funds abroad. Supposedly to make it easy for foreign investors to do business in their countries, African governments waived minimum labour and environmental standards and did not insist on minimum levels of skills transfer.

Meanwhile, in South Korea, until the late 1980s, foreign investors were not allowed majority ownership in local companies, except in very restricted circumstances. Foreign investors were restricted to sectors in which South Korea did not have the capacity, but which the country had identified as crucial for long-term development.

In the West – despite their injunctions to African nations to privatise state-owned companies in the 1970s and 1980s – very few countries actually pursued whole-scale privatisation. In Africa privatisation spawned corruption, as companies were sold off to political cronies, ethnic buddies and foreign companies that bribed local officials.

In East Asia, developing states set up development banks, run by the best brains in their countries, which financed industrialisation by providing easy credit, loans and expertise to their growing industries. In addition, they proactively identified sectors to be developed, and then built them up – rather than waiting for spontaneous development. These governments used a combination of taxation, fiscal policy, research support, tariffs and judicious foreign borrowing to develop new industries. At the same time, the import of products that could be manufactured at home and of luxury consumer goods was heavily discouraged. Companies using locally produced material were rewarded with tax rebates.

The global financial crisis has turned economic convention upside down. African countries must not be caught napping again – they must use the policy space opened by the global financial crisis to do exactly what Western nations are doing and what the East Asian states are doing once again. They must pursue relevant industrial policies and make sure that those who manage the implementation of the policies are the best talent available. Furthermore, African governments must cut out corruption and act in the broadest public interest.

Sowetan, 17 September 2009

The role of foreign banks in Africa

A dramatic new phase in China's African expansion started with its move to establish a foothold in the continent's newly resurgent financial sector. The state-owned Industrial and Commercial Bank of China (ICBC), the country's biggest lender, announced that it had purchased sizeable stakes in three African banks. It was a strategic decision: the banks were located in South Africa, the continent's biggest economy, oil-rich Nigeria, which has its largest population, and Egypt, the continent's bridge to the Middle East.

The ICBC bought a fifth of Standard Bank, Africa's biggest banking group, for $5,6 billion in cash. The Standard Bank deal is the biggest foreign acquisition by a Chinese financial institution. It will also be the largest foreign investment in Africa. With its share in Standard Bank, the Asian dragon has with one stroke grabbed a firm stake in the twenty African markets where it operates.

Of course, Africa desperately needs China's money, investments and expertise. The two most successful development efforts after the Second World War, the rebuilding of Western Europe and the rapid industrialisation of the East Asian tiger economies, could not have happened without a flood of dollars from the US. To put it into perspective, the US, between 1950 and the 1980s, poured the equivalent of all the combined aid given to 53 African countries during the same period, into just one country, South Korea. This is the kind of lift Africa needs and in our generation, China may perhaps present this kind of opportunity. But to make it work, African countries will have to be more hard-nosed about their deals. Crucially, Africans cannot again squander their strategic assets as they did during the post-independence era and again in the immediate aftermath of the end of the Cold War.

The deals African countries and companies have so far offered to China – a country that needs African commodities as badly as Africa needs the dragon's partnership – are just too soft. The Chinese economy has to maintain a 9% growth rate over the next decade, to prevent an internal implosion fuelled by ballooning domestic demand for local development, jobs and democracy. Only such growth rates can keep this at bay. But to continue to grow at head-spinning pace, China needs a deluge of affordable raw materials and at present these can only be found in Africa. So, it's almost as if history may have presented Africans, via China, with the means to take their first step on the economic ladder to future prosperity, in the way that the Marshall Plan or the US's post-war support of East Asia allowed those regions to do.

Africa has previously been deliberately marginalised by Western powers and companies. While ostensibly commiserating with the continent's various leaderships over the lot that they have inherited, they have quietly but effectively been carting away raw materials. China's new investment in Africa lays bare the oft-peddled fabrication that Africa has nothing left to offer in terms of resources, but the problem is that strategic assets are being bought up quite cheaply, under easy terms and with few obligations – most of the deals African countries have signed with China so far are outrageously skewed in China's favour.

Reserve Bank Governor Tito Mboweni is right to advise caution after the ICBC's buying of a stake in Standard Bank. The engines of the phenomenally rapid industrialisation of the East Asian tiger economies during the post-war period, certainly the most rapid industrialisation the modern world has ever seen, were their banks. At the heart of China's extraordinary development, during which it has year after year logged up economic growth rates averaging 9%, have been its banks. South Africa's banks – both state-owned and private – are the foundations on which any African recovery rests and South Africa must proceed carefully when allowing foreign companies, including China's, to buy into their domestic financial sector.

The Witness, 15 November 2007

Don't condemn Africa to underdevelopment

Is China becoming Africa's new coloniser? In what is reminiscent of a new scramble for Africa, China has rushed to plant its flag on the continent, offering soft credit, bricks-and-mortar investment and promising non-interference in local politics.

But is this all too good to be true? In November, China hosted an Africa summit in Beijing attended by 50 African leaders, the biggest showcase of China's new foreign policy shift towards the developing world. China aims to expand its political reach on the continent and secure raw materials for its rapidly growing economy. At the conference, Beijing offered Africa US$3 billion in preferential loans and US$2 billion in export credits over the next three years. China envisaged annual trade with Africa to reach US $100 billion by 2010.

Whereas Western nations such as the US, France and the United Kingdom (UK) have slashed development aid year after year, China has promised to double aid by 2009. Most of the Chinese aid to Africa is tied to business deals. Nevertheless, China has offered aid without insisting on the onerous conditions that Western donors do. This is sweet music to African nations, who for so long now have protested the hypocritical insistence of Western countries calling for Africa to open their markets while heavily subsidising their own agriculture sectors.

China earlier this year granted Nigeria a $2,5 billion soft loan and the Angolan government $9 billion without strings. But China has also offered many African despots, such as Zimbabwe's Robert Mugabe, a lifeline. China has major investments in Sudan's oilfields and fiercely supports the Sudanese regime, which is responsible for an internal conflict that has seen millions killed or displaced. China worked tirelessly to water down a UN resolution condemning Sudan for the bloodshed in Darfur. China accounts for 65% of all Sudanese oil exports and 35% of Angolan oil sold abroad. The argument can be made that many Western nations are also often quite happy to turn a blind eye to allied undemocratic regimes, especially if there are Western oil interests to protect.

Currently, most African economies depend on one or more commodities. The Chinese dragon's big appetite for commodities has given some African economies a handy windfall. Yet very few African nations have used the extra cash to diverslfy their economies. To prosper, African nations need to diversify as soon as possible. Right now, most of the rich returns from commodity sales are pocketed by a handful of African ruling elites. China's strategy of making friends by targeting leading members of African ruling parties has only encouraged this trend. The more easy money China dangles in return for oil or other commodities, the more corruption rises.

On the other hand, China's interest in Africa has given African nations more options to negotiate better trade deals with Western competitors. In the past, African countries had to accept the poor deals Western countries forced on them. In terms of global politics, many Africans do see China as a potential ally in a world where African interests are either ignored or dismissed by the big powers. As South African President Thabo Mbeki said, the continent has a 'dire need for close friends, reliable partners and good brothers'.

However, China's public altruistic rhetoric masks its hard-nosed approach. Many Africans appear not to notice this. As a case in point, China, in spite of its stated aims to make the UN more representative, has opposed the initiatives to secure a permanent seat for Africa on the UN Security Council.

In Latin America, China similarly bestowed on Brazil 'favourite nation' status but Brazil nevertheless discovered that despite this, their products faced huge tariff barriers in China. China promised to invest billions of dollars in infrastructure projects in Brazil, but this was very slow to materialise. Another sticking point was that China insisted on bringing Chinese nationals as work crews, instead of transferring skills to locals. This type of treatment already has caused sore points across Africa. Many African businesses complain that Chinese companies dump cheap end-of-the-line stock, often bypassing customs and import duties. Not only does this drive locals out of business, but the cheap items are also often of poor quality. The influx of cheap Chinese goods to Africa decimates the struggling local manufacturing industry.

In South Africa, official figures show that cheap Chinese textiles have led to the loss of at least 67 000 jobs in the past four years. South African unions have lobbied their government, who is busy negotiating a free trade deal with China to include clauses committing China to respect minimum labour, human rights and environmental standards. Most African countries, just like South Africa, export the capital-intensive commodities or raw materials that China hungers for, and import labour-intensive manufactured goods from China. So, the rise in exports to China typically generates few jobs, while imports from China take away jobs. If this continues, argues President Thabo Mbeki, the African continent could be 'condemned to underdevelopment' and 'recolonisation'. Africans should heed the warning.

The Washington Post, 7 February 2007

Broaden African elites to ensure healthy economies

The small elites which dominate politics and business are at the heart of the failures of most African countries since independence. These elites have continuously reinforced themselves over successive generations, with the aim of maintaining the status quo. As a result they have generally become richer – while the poor segments of African societies have become poorer. This has generally been the case even in African countries such as Angola – a commodity-driven economy where growth has been more robust in the past decade than for many years.

Last year, Welwitschia dos Santos, the daughter of the Angolan President José Eduardo dos Santos, no less, accused 'business oligarchs' – a few hundred people close to the president and the ruling party who control most of the country's wealth – of 'destroying' the economy. 'These business oligarchs believe they have to create the biggest number of tentacles possible to sabotage or destroy competing businesses,' she said, and added that these oligarchs 'had

enriched themselves through state funds and were stifling competition and preventing the emergence of young and honest entrepreneurs'. The irony is that Dos Santos herself became rich because
she is part of Angola's liberation aristocracy, with some of her business interests including a company that manages the country's
state-owned broadcaster.

Like Dos Santos, most of today's African elite come from the educated political class of the first independence movements, traditional
leaders or royalty. These were the power brokers under the colonial
system. In fact, in some African countries, departing colonial powers
deliberately created a small black elite, often from one ethnic group,
as part of their divide-and-rule policy. In contrast, in East Asia over
the past 50 years, since their break from colonial rule, nationalist
movements have purposefully and dramatically expanded the elite
from the same initial narrow base. This has been through specific
programmes to promote meritocracy in both the public and private
sectors.

The leadership of African independence movements generally
also became the post-independence elite in politics, business and
civil society. The newly created post-independence African middle
classes and business elite almost always developed directly out of
the political classes dominating the post-independence ruling parties. They had access to lucrative government jobs and contracts,
secured public service promotion and benefited from economic
empowerment and affirmative programmes after independence. In
those African countries that introduced economic empowerment,
affirmative action or indigenisation programmes at independence,
the beneficiaries were once again mostly from the dominant independence party and the traditional elite associated with them.

Africa's oldest liberation movement, the African National Congress (ANC) of South Africa, was conceived in 1912 by members of the educated elite, traditional leaders and royalty. This was to become the blueprint for liberation movements in Africa, and even those that were formed relatively late, such as Zimbabwe's ZANU-PF, and who started on the ideological left, were formed and dominated by the educated elite in a partnership which, in order to come to power, struck alliances in the rural areas with more conservative and traditional leadership elites. Even in the cases where independence movements were formed from trade unions or so-called more radical elements, they were still dominated by the educated elite – both FRELIMO in Mozambique and the MPLA in Angola are examples of this.

In some cases, the individuals at the helm of Africa's independence movements came from the same ethnic group, military tradition or class or attended the same school. Many of these movements actually began as ethnic, regional or culturally based organisations. Most of them, especially those on the left, did initially try to be more ethnically inclusive, yet continued to be dominated by one ethnic group when in power. In Kenya, for example, the independence leader, Jomo Kenyatta, ruled through a close-knit group consisting mostly of relatives from his native Kiambu district, members of the Kikuyu ethnic group who had been working in the colonial administration, and aligned traditional leaders.

The Cold War helped entrench the narrow African elites that had taken power after independence. Both Western and Eastern powers supported African regimes and the elites associated with them, no matter how they governed, as long as they sided with these powers in their proxy wars with their ideological opponents.

The mass democratisation of many African countries in the early 1990s saw a number of opposition parties rise to prominence and begin to challenge the old elites. But by the time the first generation of independence movements had fallen out of favour, they had given birth to a new business, government and cultural elite. So, in many instances, these new post-independence opposition parties were actually just splinters from the old political elite.

In Zimbabwe, the opposition Movement for Democratic Change (MDC) consists of both members of the old ZANU-PF elite and new entrants from the trade union movement, civil society and churches. And in Zambia, after the independence leader Kenneth Kaunda was ousted, members of the old political, business and intellectual elite struck alliances with outsiders – trade unions, civil society and churches – to form new parties. In both instances, when these newly formed opposition parties came to power – or forced the independence movements to share power – they brought new leaders into government, but did not measurably expand the elite.

In many cases the new opposition parties came to power on the basis that it was 'their time to eat', to paraphrase Kenya's former anti-corruption chief John Githongo. In African countries where the military took power forcibly from independence movements, such as The Gambia, the new rulers arose from prominent military factions and so once again failed to expand the elite base. And in those countries where dictators took control, their families and friends formed the nucleus of the new elite.

However, there are countries in Africa that have seen a marked expansion of the elite, and which have become more prosperous as a result. Although at independence, the ruling Botswana Democratic Party was dominated both by the educated elite and traditional leaders, the independence leaders there did not stand still. Botswana expanded its elite by generously providing social (education and health) services to the poor, giving the poor access to finance (especially for small farmers and small businesses) and introducing merit appointments in the public service.

In Mauritius, a breakaway from the Labour Party, the leading party of independence, less than a decade after it had come to power, led to the establishment of new parties, mostly on the left, including the Mauritian Militant Movement (MMM) – formed in 1969 in alliance with trade unions and civil society – which shook up the establishment. Not only did it force the Labour Party to genuinely govern more inclusively, but it also helped bring formerly marginalised groups into the elite.

Simply put, unless African countries expand their elites beyond the traditional status quo, they will not become prosperous.

BBC Focus on Africa magazine, July-September 2010

Make public service attractive to retain skills

Just the other day I met a black South African who studied economics up to PhD level in China. Astonishingly, he cannot find a job in the South African public service – where, alarmingly, in some provinces more than a third of all jobs are vacant.

With China's unprecedented investment safari into Africa, one would imagine then that my new acquaintance would be a prized employee in the South African public service. Yet, he says his job applications in some cases came to nought because he was either not well connected to any of the local political chiefs, or shown the door as an ethnic outsider. Sometimes, would-be employers even preferred a foreign consultant.

Sadly, my friend's case is an example of a very common phenomenon across our continent. Globally, nations are producing fewer doctors, engineers and nurses. It is often said that developed nations lure skilled professionals away from developing countries, and make it, as South African Finance Minister Trevor Manuel phrased it, 'more difficult or impossible for developing countries to reduce poverty and attain their development goals.'

But it is undoubtedly a mistake to believe that only Western countries are to blame for the brain drain from African and other developing countries. Or that skilled Africans only take up the opportunities offered to them because of higher wages in these industrialised countries.

For starters, the unstable political environments in many African countries – Kenya and Zimbabwe are cases in point – are hardly conducive to keeping the best brains at home. Furthermore, considerations other than proficiency and skills more often than not influence appointments to positions in government and sometimes even local private companies. For example, how close you are to local party bosses, or your ethnicity, is often more crucial in a job application than your qualifications.

African governments do not appear to value the skills of their own nationals. They will use costly foreign experts, who are parachuted in from outside, even if they have capable ones at home who are more likely to be in tune with local realities.

Take the case of South Africa. Throughout his term, President Thabo Mbeki has used outside economists to formulate and assess economic policies. Nothing wrong with that, but as Iraj Abedian, the former chief economist of Standard Bank says, there are perfectly capable local economists, who know the South African economy much more intimately.

One reason for the dizzying economic success of countries such as South Korea is that they adopted merit-based systems of appointment in public administration. In the long run, unless political parties, government departments and private companies are run on merit, rather than along tribal or political lines, Africa's scarce skills won't stay home.

BBC World Service Letter from Africa radio column, 14 January 2008

Crisis hits poor countries hardest

As the US, Europe and rich countries throw billions at the financial crisis – in an attempt to end it – spare a thought for poorer developing nations, who without such means are facing absolute disaster.

For many developing countries, already battling to contain food shortages and high fuel prices, the spillover from the financial crisis that started in rich nations will stunt growth and development for perhaps a generation. Very few developing countries can effectively tackle the effects of the financial crisis, because they lack the resources at the disposal of richer nations, and it is likely to unleash waves of social instability.

Going forward, rich nations will have to plug the holes the multi-billion rescue packages have left in their treasuries, and it is inevitable that some of this will be done with money that would have gone towards development and aid commitments. Furthermore, a credit freeze in Western countries, caused by the fall in confidence because of the financial crisis, means that money generally available to finance economic projects in developing countries will now dry up. If rich nations are starting to feel the pinch (factory and company closures), imagine what will happen in the economies of developing countries.

One of the reasons for the financial crisis is that the financial, trade and political systems that underpin the world economy are outdated. In fact, this crisis offers a unique opportunity to overhaul the IMF, the World Bank, the World Trade Organisation (WTO) and the UN, to make them more relevant. It is instructive to note that Iceland, facing unprecedented bankruptcy because of the financial crisis, turned down help from the IMF, and even considered seeking support from Russia. The financial crisis has discredited the laissez-faire 'free market' model of capitalism. International financial institutions, such as the World Bank and IMF, have long espoused this model as a one-size-fits-all solution to creating growth in vulnerable developing countries. Those who followed such advice are now the worse off for doing so.

If there is anything close to a silver lining in this crisis, it is this: many developing countries for some time now have complained that they lacked the freedom to come up with economic policies appropriate to their own circumstances. For example, before this crisis, if the few developing countries with the means to do so had used public money to bail out struggling banks as the US and EU have done, they would have faced a market backlash. After this financial crisis, developing countries may now have more freedom to come up with their own economic policies.

The short-term solution to the financial crisis is a concerted global effort to restore confidence. This will mean correcting market failures – by providing public support (as the US, UK and Europe have done). But there also has to be an international financial facility that can step in to prop up institutions which, if they failed, would plunge an economy into bankruptcy. Access to this facility must be made available to developing countries without them having to give up their ability to set their own economic policies, as has been the case in the past when they turned to the IMF and World Bank for help.

In the long term, both industrialised and developing countries will have to come up with a collective strategy that will transform the current outdated global financial, trade and political architecture. Both groups will have to be involved in writing new and more appropriate rules and regulations. From now on there will have to be better regulation and supervision to improve the functioning of financial markets, both at national and global levels.

This is not just a financial crisis, it is a moral crisis. So far Western governments have bailed out banks, but not punished those responsible. Hard-working citizens have lost a great deal and will continue to lose out – pensions, homes and savings have all been thrown under the proverbial bus. Those individuals who caused this crisis did so simply out of greed. To allow them to get away with this (for example, still receiving huge executive payouts) while millions suffer from their irresponsible behaviour compounds the moral failure.

The Washington Post, 20 October 2008

Wealth *for* Africa, not *from* Africa

The aftereffects of the global financial crisis may lead to the re-colonisation of some African countries, with some likely to go bankrupt while others are stripped of their assets by Western and Eastern powers. The signs of Africa's re-colonisation are ominous and action is needed quickly; there is no time to dilly-dally, shout slogans or blame imperialist forces. We must come up with effective responses.

There are already plans to link the hydroelectric dam project in the Democratic Republic of Congo (DRC) to southern Europe. The project has the backing of the World Bank, despite the fact that less than 10% of Congolese people have access to electricity and, indeed, continent-wide the United Nations Development Programme (UNDP) figures show that less than 30% of Africans have access to electricity.

In August this year, the EU signed an agreement with Nigeria, Niger and Algeria to build a pipeline that will channel gas directly to Europe. Again, Nigeria, Niger and Algeria cannot even supply gas to their own citizens.

In July this year, a consortium of European companies announced that they would build a facility in the Sahara Desert that will produce enough solar power to satisfy 15% of Europe's energy needs by 2050.

Western and Eastern governments and multinationals are increasingly also buying African land to set up commercial agricultural businesses from which they export products back to their own countries or to other markets. A South Korean multinational bought fertile land in Madagascar and Sudan at a pittance; Indian farming companies have fertile lands in Ethiopia, Kenya, Madagascar, Senegal and Mozambique; Chinese companies are also buying tracts of land for agricultural purposes.

A report by the UN Food and Agriculture Organisation (FAO) stated that more than 2,5 million hectares of African land had been bought by foreign companies since 2004, and this is only scratching the surface. Yet most African countries now import food.

Similarly, foreign companies are also buying up African mines on the cheap, as African countries fail to come up with economic strategies to deal with the devastating effects of the global financial crisis. Western and Asian countries are buying up African minerals to buttress global commodity price fluctuations. They are looking for strategic commodities, including platinum, oil and gas.

African countries must now stop selling off their assets and increase trade with one another. We must stop simply exporting raw materials, a practice that doesn't generate large-scale employment, and instead beneficiate and diversify. We need to pool our money, knowledge and expertise.

We will need effective leadership and to jettison the likes of Robert Mugabe. Furthermore, we must boost the quality of our democracies and cobble together industrial policies through developmental coalitions between governments, communities, businesses and civil societies. Finally, African countries should promptly form a continental common market and political union, underpinned by democracy.

Sowetan, 10 September 2009

Copenhagen is a disaster for Africa

Climate change is frequently a matter of life and death for many Africans. From whatever angle you look at it, the climate change 'deal' that was bulldozed through by rich nations at the Copenhagen climate conference was a disaster for Africa. Compared with rich nations who dictated the terms of the 'deal', African countries contribute the least to greenhouse emissions. However, they suffer the consequences the most. African nations will again disproportionally feel the pinch of this deal.

All the PR coming thick and fast from the architects of the Copenhagen deal will not ease the real-life impact of climate change on Africa: water shortages, hunger and the possible disappearance of entire island states at risk of being submerged because of rising sea levels. In September this year, the UN Food and Agricultural Organisation (FAO) warned that poor crops, forced migration and conflict will drive millions more people to starvation across the continent. Food production has been plummeting across Africa because of increasingly irregular rainfall.

In Uganda, this year the country will post its fourth successive poor harvest of first-season crops. In countries such as Somalia, half of the population now depends on food aid. Many nomadic peoples in East Africa are in a battle for survival because of increasingly severe and frequent droughts. New conflicts are arising in places such as Uganda, northern Kenya and Ethiopia, this time over access to increasingly rapidly diminishing water sources.

The World Bank, in its April 2009 report 'Sea-level Rise and Storm Surges: a Comparative Analysis of Impacts in Developing Countries', in which it compared population, economic and elevation maps to analyse countries most at risk from rising sea levels, identified ten

African countries as the most vulnerable to storm surges. Islands are particularly at risk: the Seychelles fear that they may lose 60% of their land because of rising sea levels. In southwestern Uganda, temperatures have risen so much that there is now a real danger of the return of old pests such as malaria, and the outbreak of new ones. Staple crops such as soya and cassava are at risk.

It is not surprising then that countries such as Sudan, Ethiopia and Ghana rejected the final Copenhagen conference document in the strongest terms possible. Lumumba Di-Aping, the lead Sudanese negotiator, said the deal was 'devoid of any sense of responsibility or morality'.

Many Africans were convinced that the final text was cobbled together by rich nations long before the start of the conference. The role of Africans was to turn up, rubber-stamp it and then appear, smiling, next to leaders of the rich countries as props at the photoshoots later. This suspicion was confirmed at the start of the conference when a leaked Danish document proposed that industrial nations cut fewer emissions, while the developing world should face tougher limits on greenhouse gases. This outraged African negotiators and activists so much that many stormed out of the meeting room.

The final 'deal', signed by 28 countries, kicked aside a UN-brokered deal that was more inclusive, financially more generous and more sensitive to the needs of African and developing countries – and which was backed by Africans. In Copenhagen, industrial nations have again successfully managed to divide African and developing countries, by co-opting the bigger developing countries, such as China, India, Brazil and South Africa, in private deals.

Such co-opting often starts with the demonising of these countries: those who insist on a fair deal are being mercilessly portrayed as stubborn obstacles in the march for a greener future, or as much to blame for global problems as industrial nations, and therefore should make the same compromises – and pay for it also. Of course, the big developing countries – China, India, Brazil and South Africa – are not blameless when it comes to polluting the earth.

Industrial nations also isolated certain African nations into allying with them, either by promising or withdrawing future aid. That is why Sudan and Ethiopia, among the African countries that stand to lose the most from this bad deal, were there among those signing the accord, although they afterwards attacked it as unfair.

African countries lack the money and access to technology – restricted by patent laws in industrial nations – to counter the effects of climate change, or to build green economies. The offer of $100 billion a year by 2020 to be financed by governments and the private sector not only ridiculously lacks the detail, it is simply inadequate. The big fear among African nations is that the financial mathematics to finance the deal is all a con: industrial nations will just transfer existing aid commitments to this fund, as they did before. It is not surprising that the deal is rather vague on just how the private sector is going to partially finance African and developing countries' efforts to overcome the effects of climate change – as it proposes.

It is imperative that African and developing countries understand that progressive efforts to tackle climate change in Africa and the developing world are unlikely to happen, unless there is also a parallel reform of the global political, trade and finance rules.

Yet Africans can also take some good from this climate talk failure. In spite of the divide-and-rule tactics of industrial nations, there are positive signs that African countries may yet be able to unite in seeking solutions to important global problems that affect them. Africans need such a genuine common union.

Civil society groups in these countries will have to provide the intellectual leadership that is lacking among the political leaders. The political leaders who led the African delegations, many of them ruling their own countries undemocratically, did their countries a disservice.

In African countries, civil society, together with ordinary citizens and communities, must keep the pressure on their leaders and hold them accountable. They must start national conversations in which their governments must account for what happened in Copenhagen, and how to rectify it.

In industrial countries, civil society organisations and individuals must expose their leaders' bullying of African countries to their citizens and unmask the blame-shifting (to developing countries) used by their leaders to cover up the bullying. A failed climate change deal is not only bad for citizens of African and developing countries – it is for industrial nations, too.

The Guardian, 23 December 2009

Acknowledgements

The author acknowledges with thanks the following publications in which his columns, opinion pieces and blogs have appeared: *Sowetan*, *The Witness*, *Sunday Independent*, *Sunday Times*, *Mail & Guardian*, *Beeld*, *Rapport*, *Business Day*, *Cape Times*, *The Washington Post*, *Newsweek* (New York), *The Times* (London), *The Guardian* (London), *The Independent* (London), *New Statesman* (London), *The Financial Times* (London), *BBC World Service Business Daily*, *BBC Focus on Africa* magazine, Reuters, *SA Reconciliation Barometer*, *Open Space* magazine, *ARISE* magazine (London), *ZAM* magazine (Amsterdam), *Global Briefing* (Cambridge), *Pambazuka News* (Oxford) and the Economist Intelligence Unit (London). Lots of appreciation to the energy, enthusiasm and dedication of publisher Annie Olivier and her colleagues at Tafelberg who helped make this collection possible.

Index

World We're In, The, 99

xenophobia, 89, 91-92, 128, 168

Yengeni, Tony, 185

Zanufication, 235-236
ZANU-PF, 17, 139, 148, 230, 233-236, 238, 255-256
Zille, Helen, 50, 155, 158

Zimbabwe, 17, 89, 147-148, 214, 216, 218-220, 228, 230-239, 251, 255-256, 258
Zokwana, Senzeni, 185
Zuma, Jacob, 16, 18, 20-21, 23-25, 27-29, 34, 42, 49-51, 53-79, 84, 87-88, 104, 109, 119-120, 122, 124-125, 127, 133, 138, 140, 163, 166, 171, 173-174, 178, 180, 183, 186-188, 199, 205-206, 231

www.ingramcontent.com/pod-product-compliance
Lightning Source LLC
Chambersburg PA
CBHW031426270326
41930CB00007B/591

* 9 7 8 0 6 2 4 0 5 5 9 2 1 *